① DramaScripts

ADRIAN FLYNN

DE STANDERLINE

OXFORD
UNIVERSITY PRESS

OXFORD
UNIVERSITY PRESS

Great Clarendon Street, Oxford OX2 6DP

Oxford University Press is a department of the University of Oxford.
It furthers the University's objective of excellence in research,
scholarship, and education by publishing worldwide in

Oxford   New York

Auckland   Cape Town   Dar es Salaam   Hong Kong   Karachi
Kuala Lumpur   Madrid   Melbourne   Mexico City   Nairobi
New Delhi   Shanghai   Taipei   Toronto

With offices in

Argentina   Austria   Brazil   Chile   Czech Republic   France   Greece
Guatemala   Hungary   Italy   Japan   Poland   Portugal   Singapore
South Korea   Switzerland   Thailand   Turkey   Ukraine   Vietnam

Oxford is a registered trade mark of Oxford University Press
in the UK and in certain other countries

Dramascripts 1: Exchanges © Adrian Flynn, Joe Standerline 2006
Activities © Martin Lewis, John Rainer 2006

The moral rights of the author have been asserted

Database right Oxford University Press (maker)

First published 2006

All rights reserved. No part of this publication may be reproduced,
stored in a retrieval system, or transmitted, in any form or by any means,
without the prior permission in writing of Oxford University Press, or as
expressly permitted by law, or under terms agreed with the appropriate
reprographics rights organization. Enquiries concerning reproduction
outside the scope of the above should be sent to the Rights Department,
Oxford University Press, at the address above

You must not circulate this book in any other binding or cover
and you must impose this same condition on any acquirer

British Library Cataloguing in Publication Data

Data available

ISBN-13: 978-0-19-832181-1
ISBN-10: 0-19-832181-3

10 9 8 7 6 5 4 3 2 1

Printed and bound by Creative Print and Design Wales, Ebbw Vale.

By Adrian Flynn
Mexico
The Corridor
Goodnight, Night owl
Siege
Coming to terms

By Joe Standerline
She's behind you
Delinquent
Boy band
Helen's kitchen
Going nowhere

Contents

Introduction	5
Mexico	6
The Corridor	24
Goodnight, Night owl	40
Siege	58
Coming to terms	75
She's behind you	95
Delinquent	123
Boy band	142
Helen's kitchen	156
Going nowhere	186

Introduction

Welcome to *Oxford Dramascripts!*

Oxford Dramascripts are collections of thought-provoking extracts and short plays especially selected or commissioned to provide a source of fresh, relevant material that will meet the practical needs of all GCSE Drama students.

Each Dramascripts volume features ten scripts and covers a wide range of compelling themes and challenging issues. Cast sizes vary between three and eight actors and the scripts last between 15 and 40 minutes respectively, making them ideal for use in examined performance.

Every script is followed by a double-page spread of explorative, thought-provoking activities, carefully designed to tease out questions raised by the text and providing stimulating insights into the writing. The activities will act as a springboard for more detailed work on each piece and whet the appetite for further study.

In this volume, *Exchanges*, you will find ten specially commissioned plays covering a variety of themes – including family dynamics, war, delinquency and sexuality – and exploring a range of theatrical styles. Designed to engage interest and spark further explorative work, this volume provides inspiring opportunities for performance.

Mexico

Characters

Colin	A businessman, in his 40s
Margery	His wife, also in her 40s
Dawn	Their daughter, aged 15
Tom	Dawn's twin brother
Charlotte	A school friend of Tom and Dawn

The play is set on the shingle beach of a British coastal resort during the summer holidays. The beach is deserted and a strong breeze is blowing.

Margery comes on laden with bags, and is almost knocked down by a gust of wind. As the wind dies down, she regains her balance and looks round.

Margery [*Beckoning offstage*] Colin, Colin! Quick!

Colin staggers on clutching four fold-up chairs and a windbreak.

Hurry!

Colin What's the rush?

Margery In case anyone else grabs this spot.

Colin [*Disbelieving*] There's no one around for miles. It's the windiest, shingliest corner of the beach.

He puts the chairs down in a pile and starts setting up the windbreak.

Margery [*Beckoning off*] Dawnie, Tommy, we've found somewhere.

Colin We might bump into a couple of penguins, but not much else. I told you it was a waste of time coming on holiday.

Margery Please don't start again. [*To* **Tom**, *offstage*] Hurry up!

MEXICO

Tom *struggles on with an enormously heavy picnic basket. He's wearing brightly coloured beach shorts and designer sunglasses. He puts the basket down and shivers.*

Tom   We're not stopping here, are we?

Margery It's lovely, Tommy!

Tom   Tom.

Colin   [*Trying to stabilize the windbreak*] Give us a hand, son. We need some protection from the arctic conditions.

Dawn comes on wearing a thick coat, scarf and woolly hat. She's carrying a shoulder bag full of books.

Dawn   How I am supposed to work on my science module here? It's blowing a gale!

Margery Dawnie? Have you dropped something?

Dawn looks down, tuts with annoyance and goes back offstage. Margery starts rummaging through her bags. Colin and Tom finish erecting the windbreak. Tom shivers.

Colin   [*To Tom*] Aren't you cold?

Tom   No. I'm all right.

Margery I've brought your jumper from the hotel, Tommy.

She extracts an embarrassingly unstylish jumper from a carrier bag.

Tom   No thanks.

Margery Sure?

Tom   Certain.

Margery puts the jumper back in the bag. Colin picks up the fold-up chairs as Dawn comes back on carrying a large inflatable lilo.

Dawn   I dropped it by the mini-trampolines.

She drops the lilo and her bag of books.

Margery I expect you two'll want a go on those later.

Dawn   The trampolines?

7

Tom	Puh-lease…
Margery	Well, you always used to.
Colin	[*Handing out chairs*] We might as well sit down, since your mother's insisted we come and enjoy ourselves.
	As all four try to set up their chairs, the wind picks up again. In balletic slow motion, they struggle to control the chairs — which threaten to blow away or even lift them off the ground — until the wind suddenly dies down. As the chairs crash to the ground, **Colin**, **Margery**, **Tom** *and* **Dawn** *fall into sitting positions in them.* **Tom** *and* **Dawn** *sit slightly apart from their parents.*
Margery	A breath of sea air's so refreshing, isn't it?
Tom	Can we have the picnic now?
Margery	Later, Tommy.
Tom	Tom!
Margery	We've only just got here. I expect we all want a swim first.
	Colin, **Dawn** *and* **Tom** *gaze in horror at the sea.*
Colin	The Titanic went down in warmer than that.
	He shakes his head and takes an electronic organiser from his bag.
Margery	Perhaps you're right. Let's get the postcards out of the way.
	Margery *rummages in her bag for a pen and postcards.* **Dawn** *takes a textbook from her shoulder bag.* **Tom** *stretches out to maximise a possible suntan, despite shivering with cold.*
Dawn	Stop shivering, I need to concentrate.
Tom	I can't help it. It's freezing.
Margery	Dawnie, that's not a textbook, is it?
Dawn	It certainly is. [*Opening the book*] The Human Tribe, by Dr Ronald Stote. I've got exams to prepare for.
Margery	Your GCSEs aren't for a year yet.

Dawn	[*Tapping the book*] 'The most successful individuals in any society are those who plan ahead.' It says so in here. That's why I've produced an action plan. [*She takes a long, complex roll of paper from her pocket*] Science this morning, maths this afternoon, and a mock exam paper this evening when the rest of you go to karaoke.
Margery	But we're on holiday.
Dawn	You lot might be. If I'm to become a psychologist, I need to study. I want to succeed when I go back to school. Not like Tom.
Tom	I'll do all right.
Dawn	Dr Stote says 'overconfidence and under-preparation are the hallmarks of immature male members of the troupe'.
	She starts reading.
Tom	[*Unimpressed*] Oh, does he?
Margery	[*To* **Dawn**] Half an hour only. We're here to switch off. You don't see your father thinking about the office, do you?
	She turns to **Colin** *who is engrossed in reading his e-mails.*
Colin	We're going to lose the Glasgow order if we're not careful. I should have been there to take care of it.
Margery	[*To* **Colin**] You're not going to worry about work all week, are you?
Colin	I might not have a job to go back to at this rate. I must send some e-mails.
Margery	Relax, Colin. Enjoy the view.
Colin	[*Looks up*] The oil refinery looks particularly spectacular this year. Now, excuse me.
	He returns to his personal organiser. **Tom** *shivers.* **Margery** *takes the embarrassing jumper out of the bag.*
Margery	Tommy?
Tom	No thanks. I'm lovely and warm.

MEXICO

Puzzled, **Margery** puts the jumper back and tries to compose the first postcard. **Tom** shivers again.

Dawn   [Quietly, to **Tom**] If you're so cold, why don't you put a shirt on?

Tom   [Quietly] Because I need a suntan.

Dawn   A suntan? What for?

Tom   I just do.

He shifts round in his chair to catch more of the very weak sun. **Dawn** shakes her head and returns to her book.

Margery   [To **Colin**] What shall I say to your mother?

Colin   [Not looking up] Hello, Mum.

Margery   Oh, Colin. You know she loves getting postcards from us. Though she'd like a visit even better.

Colin   How often do I have to tell you, Margery? I can't take any more time off work. It's bad enough coming on holiday now. Jenkins in finance is after my job. He may pounce any minute.

He returns to his personal organiser. **Tom** shivers.

Dawn   [Looking up from her book, irritated] Why are you so desperate for a suntan?

Tom   I just am.

Dawn   [Insistent] But why?

Tom   [Reluctantly] Because…

Dawn   Yes…?

Tom   Because I'm in Mexico.

Dawn   No you're not.

Tom   Yes, I am.

Dawn   The sub-zero temperature is a pretty big clue we're still in Britain. [Beginning to understand] Unless… Why do you think you're in Mexico?

MEXICO

Tom   [*With an embarrassed shrug*] I dunno.

Dawn   It's your big mouth again, isn't it? You've told someone you're going there for your holiday!

Tom   No. [*Pause*] Well…

Dawn   Angelina Davis! You said it to impress her, didn't you?

Tom   No!

Dawn   I bet you did. You've gone bright red.

Tom   I haven't.

Dawn   You have. [*Quoting from her book*] 'Social embarrassment causes the small blood vessels of the face to dilate.' You're as dilated as a beetroot.

Tom   I only said it to prove her wrong.

Dawn   About what?

Tom   She called me a boring wuss who'd never been anywhere or done anything. So I told her I was spending all summer in Acapulco at my friend Juan's beach hut.

Dawn   You haven't got a friend called Juan.

Tom   And he hasn't got a beach hut either. But when I said it, Angelina looked at me sort of…

Dawn   How?

Tom   With respect. Like she might even go out with me next term, if I come back with exotic tales of all-night beach parties and a golden, glowing tan.

Dawn   You're paler than a bottle of milk.

Tom   I know. [*Shivering*] And I'm freezing.

             He turns to face the sun. **Dawn** *returns to her book.*

Margery [*Putting down her pen*] How does this sound? [*Reading aloud from the postcard*] 'Dear Mum, we're back having a great time in Little Windy.' [*Looking up*] Can you believe, we've been coming here for over twelve years?

Dawn	[*Without looking up*] Easily.
Colin	[*Without looking up*] Seems longer.
Margery	[*Continuing to read*] 'The hotel's very nice, even if the rooms are a little small.'
Colin	[*Without looking up*] They've put us in the broom cupboard.
Margery	'The good news is, we're a lot further away from the car park than last year, so hardly got woken up at all last night. We've been lucky with the weather as well so far. There's a lovely sea-breeze to stop us overheating…'
Tom	Huh!
Margery	'…and a great night's karaoke to look forward to tonight.'
	Tom, Colin and **Dawn** *all groan.*
Margery	'Well, that's all for now. Lots of love, Colin, Margery, Dawnie and Tommy.'
Tom	Tom!
Margery	[*To* **Colin**] What do you think?
Colin	[*Without looking up*] I think I'll have a sandwich.
Tom	Me, too.
Margery	Why not? After all, we're on holiday. How about you Dawnie?
Dawn	[*Without looking up*] Malnourished members of the tribe rarely function at full capacity.
Tom	She means – yes.
	Margery *opens the picnic hamper and starts putting sandwiches on plates.*
Colin	[*Glancing offstage*] There's another idiot finally risking this end of the beach.
Dawn	[*Intrigued*] Notice the territorial behaviour. She's not coming too close, in case she triggers a display of aggression. But you can tell she's interested by the glances she's giving.
Margery	[*Handing* **Colin** *a sandwich on a plate*] Colin.
Tom	Who are you talking about?

MEXICO

Colin	The lass down by the groyne. She looks about your age.
Margery	[Handing **Dawn** a plate] Dawnie.
Tom	[Looking off, horrified] Oh, no! It's Charlotte Welby.
Dawn	Angelina's best friend?
Tom	Yes. She's bound to tell Angelina she's seen me here. Then Angelina'll tell the whole school I didn't go to Mexico. I'll be humiliated.
Dawn	Too right. You'll have to walk round with a bag over your head.
Tom	Cheers.
	He grabs the lilo and tries to hide behind it.
Margery	[Passing a plate without looking up] Tommy.
	Tom puts one arm round the lilo and takes the plate.
	Who are we talking about?
Dawn	A member of Tom's social sub-group. Charlotte Welby.
Colin	How come you've never mentioned her? She's quite a looker.
Margery	She'll be company for you, Tommy. [Calls off] Hello, Charlotte!
Tom	[Behind lilo] Mum!
Margery	[To **Tom**] What on earth are you doing?
Tom	[Behind lilo] She mustn't see me.
Margery	Why not?
Dawn	He's committed a small deception to impress a potential partner of perceived higher status.
Margery	Pardon?
Dawn	He's in Mexico.
Margery	Don't be silly. [Pulls the lilo away] He's here. [Calls off] Hello, Charlotte!
	Charlotte enters.

13

MEXICO

Charlotte Hello, Dawn. [*To* **Tom**] Hi.

Tom gives an embarrassed wave and says nothing.

Margery I'm Margery and this is Colin. Tommy and Dawnie's parents. Come and sit down, love. It's always nice meeting their friends.

Charlotte You don't mind?

Colin Be our guest. [*Sarcastically*] If you can stand the excitement.

He returns to his personal organiser.

Tom [*Hurriedly*] Charlotte's probably got loads of other things to do.

Charlotte I haven't, actually. Mum and Dad are… [*searching for the right word*] busy. So I've come for a walk.

Margery Would you like a sandwich, Charlotte?

Charlotte No thanks. I haven't got much of an appetite at the moment.

Margery Tommy, give her your chair.

Tom [*Out of the corner of his mouth*] Tom!

Margery [*To* **Tom**] You can sit on the lilo.

Tom *stands up.*

Charlotte You honestly don't mind me joining you?

Dawn As long as you don't disturb my studies.

She starts reading again. **Tom** *passes* **Charlotte** *his chair. There's a sudden gust of wind and she has to battle to keep hold of it.* **Tom**'s *lilo is blown towards a corner of the stage.* **Tom** *catches it, thinks about rejoining the others, then decides to sit away from them.* **Charlotte** *wonders where to sit.*

Margery [*Pointing towards where* **Tom** *is sitting*] You'll be more out of the wind over there, love.

Charlotte *takes her chair over to sit near* **Tom**. *They exchange sideways glances, unsure of how to start a conversation.*

Tom [*Blurts out*] You're probably wondering why…

14

MEXICO

Charlotte	[*At the same time*] I really hope I'm not…
	They both stop talking, embarrassed.
	After you, Tom.
Tom	No. You first.
Charlotte	I hope I'm not being a nuisance, that's all.
Tom	No. Not really.
Charlotte	Oh, good. Only I've been walking on my own for the last hour and, well, I was getting lonely.
Tom	Your parents don't make you hang around with them?
Charlotte	They prefer it if I don't.
Tom	You don't know how lucky you are.
Charlotte	They can row better with no one else listening.
Tom	[*Surprised*] Oh.
Charlotte	What were you going to say?
Tom	You're, er… probably wondering why I'm not in Mexico.
Charlotte	[*Surprised*] Er… no. No, I'm not.
Tom	Oh. Good.
	Their conversation drops into an embarrassed silence. Across the stage, **Margery** *taps* **Colin**'s *arm.*
Colin	[*Looking up in annoyance*] What?
Margery	[*Quietly, indicating* **Tom** *and* **Charlotte**] Look.
Colin	At what?
Margery	Tom. That's how you used to look at me when we started courting.
Colin	[*Returning to his work*] I hadn't seen so much of you then.
Tom	[*To* **Charlotte**] You see, the reason I thought you'd think I was in Mexico… That's where I told your best mate I was going to be.

15

Charlotte Who do you mean?

Tom Angelina Davies.

Charlotte She's no mate of mine. Not any more.

Tom No?

Charlotte And why did you tell her you're in Mexico?

Tom Because... well, because...

Charlotte Do you fancy her?

Tom [Hurriedly] No. [Surprised to realize this is actually the truth] No, I don't.

Charlotte I wouldn't blame you. Most lads do. She's really attractive. But she bad-mouths everyone.

Tom I know.

Charlotte Some of the things she said about Mum and Dad splitting up were awful.

Tom Your parents are splitting up?

Charlotte Yeah.

Tom I didn't know. That's tough.

He moves closer to **Charlotte***. They smile shyly at each other and fall quiet, not sure how to continue the conversation. Meanwhile, across the stage:*

Margery [Whispering] Colin!

Colin [Looks up, irritated] What?

Margery Look at them now.

Colin What's happening?

Margery What do you think?

Colin [Not interested] Oh.

Margery Remember when we first got together?

Colin [Without looking up] 'Course I do. You've not stopped talking since.

MEXICO

Margery   [*Fondly*] Our first time here. The only time I ever went on a school trip.

Colin   [*Looking up*] And what a mess you made of it. You could've broken your leg tumbling out of that bus.

Margery   No chance.

Colin   Eh?

Margery   Have you never wondered how I landed so perfectly in your arms?

Colin   What?

Margery mimes an elegant fall.

You mean…?

Margery signals him to be quiet. Across the stage, Charlotte begins to talk again.

Charlotte   You see, coming on holiday was meant to be a last chance for them to sort things out.

Tom   Right.

Charlotte   But it's been a total disaster. They rowed in the car all the way here; they had another go at each other over breakfast this morning. Everyone in our hotel looked round to see what was going off.

Tom   How embarrassing.

Charlotte   I don't mind being embarrassed if it helps them stay together. But it doesn't. They're like two boats getting blown further and further apart. They don't understand what each other's saying, so they just start shouting louder. It only makes it worse. I cleared off this morning because I'd had enough. I thought a walk along the beach would clear my head. But it hasn't.

Tom   Sounds awful.

He looks sympathetically at Charlotte, half reaches out his arm to her, then pulls it away, embarrassed.

Colin   [*Whispering, unable to contain himself any longer*] It was deliberate?!

Margery   Of course it was. I'd been practising that fall for weeks.

Colin   [*Shocked*] You almost knocked me flat.

17

MEXICO

Margery	You didn't seem to mind.
Colin	I was being a gentleman.
Margery	Is that why you stuck with me for the rest of the day?
Colin	I was making sure you were all right, that's all.
Margery	[*Teasing*] Is that the only reason?
Colin	It's so long ago, I can hardly remember.
Margery	[*Whispering*] Dawnie!

She draws **Dawn's** *attention to* **Tom** *and* **Charlotte**. *Across the stage:*

Charlotte	Angelina says I'm stupid to care. People break up all the time, I shouldn't let it bother me. But it does. They're my family. My life. [*Short pause*] When we go back, Mum's moving out. Says she's found someone else. And, of course, Angelina had to stick the knife in about that.
Tom	How?
Charlotte	She says Dad's so boring, it's no wonder my mother wants shot of him. But he's not boring. He's my dad and this is breaking his heart. [*On the verge of tears*] I'm sorry.
Tom	It's all right, Charlotte.

He moves closer and circles his arm round her shoulder, but then draws it away without touching her.

Margery	[*Quietly, to* **Colin**] That's exactly how you were with me. Unsure of yourself. That's why I gave you a little kiss for encouragement.
Colin	[*Remembering*] That's right. Quite a good kiss, actually. [*Starting to relax*] And then we went in the amusements together.
Margery	You lost all your money, so I had to buy you your candy floss.
Colin	I've been paying you back ever since.
Margery	And do you remember how the trip finished?
Colin	Aye.

18

Margery	Us sitting on the cliff top, when we should have been running back to the bus.
Colin	The sun shining, yachts on the water, [*pause*] and a pretty lass sat next to me. This seemed the best place in the world then.
Margery	It still does to me. When we stop and notice.
Colin	[*Touched*] Do you mean that?

Tom *clears his throat.* **Colin** *puts his personal organiser down and leans forward to listen.*

Tom	[*Awkwardly*] I'm real sorry about your parents, Charlotte.
Charlotte	It's all right.
Tom	No, I am. Mine are a total pain. But I'm used to them by now. And I'd hate them splitting up.

Dawn *scuttles over to* **Colin** *and* **Margery** *carrying her book.*

Dawn	[*Quietly*] It's absolutely fascinating. They've moved beyond sideways glances and looking away. Now they're making prolonged eye contact and permitting each other into their personal space.
Colin	What are you on about, Dawn?
Dawn	[*Tapping the book*] They're signalling a mutual attraction. Any time now, Dr Stote says their hands will make contact.

Margery and Colin
Ssh!

They all lean further forward and listen intently to **Charlotte** *and* **Tom***'s conversation.*

Charlotte	By the way, I'm in Brazil, if you see Angelina.
Tom	Brazil?
Charlotte	With her saying Dad was boring, I told her he was taking me to the rainforest this summer. At the moment, I'm meant to be hacking my way through the undergrowth with a machete.
Tom	I'm glad you're not.

MEXICO

Charlotte Me too.

Tom [*Short pause*] It's not too bad here, is it? Except for the weather... and the beach ... and everything.

Charlotte It's all right.

Tom The sea's nice. Cold, but nice.

Charlotte Yes. And there's a smart new beach café further down.

Tom Is there?

Charlotte I passed it this morning. [*Pause*] I wouldn't mind seeing what it's like.

Tom Oh?

Colin [*Quietly*] Come on, Tom.

Margery [*Quietly*] Come on, Tommy.

Dawn [*Fairly quietly*] Get on with it.

Tom [*Summoning up courage*] So...

Charlotte Yes?

Tom Do you...

Charlotte Yes?

Tom Do you...

Charlotte What?

Tom ...think it'll get sunny later?

Dawn [*Exploding*] For heaven's sake! This is a mating ritual not a weather forecast. Ask her out!

Everyone looks at **Dawn**.

Sorry. Don't mind me.

Tom Do you want to go for a coffee, Charlotte?

Charlotte I'd love to.

20

MEXICO

Tom	Great!
	They get up. **Colin** *and* **Margery** *hurriedly pretend they haven't been listening.*
	Me and Charlotte are going to the café.
Margery	[Innocently] Are you? How nice. What about taking your jumper?
	Margery *starts taking the embarrassing jumper out of its bag.* **Colin** *hurriedly shoves it back before* **Charlotte** *can see it.*
Colin	[Quietly, to **Margery**] Give the lad a chance. [To **Tom**] No need to rush back.
Tom	We won't.
Charlotte	[Holds her hand out to **Tom**] Come on, then.
	Tom, *in a happy daze, takes* **Charlotte's** *hand.* **Dawn** *punches the air in triumph.*
Dawn	[To herself] Yes!
	Tom *and* **Charlotte** *exit.*
	Dr Stote's a genius. He'll get me through my exams.
	She takes off her scarf and woolly hat and sits down happily to resume reading. **Colin** *and* **Margery** *look at each other contentedly for a moment.*
Margery	Do you know what I think?
Colin	What?
Margery	It'd be nice to visit Mexico and Brazil one day, when we've got the time.
Colin	Wouldn't it?
Margery	But for now, this'll do.
Colin	Aye. It's not so bad here.
	He holds his hand out to her and she takes it.
	Blackout.

21

MEXICO

Group activities

1. Have you ever been on holiday, or for a day trip, to one of the British seaside resorts? What can you remember of it? Make a list of the different elements of a traditional British seaside holiday. As a sequence of still images with narration, create a guide to the British seaside holiday in the style of a TV holiday show featuring 'exotic' locations.

2. Improvise a scene which takes place back at school after the holiday. Angelina approaches Tom in the playground. Start the scene as Angelina asks Tom, 'So, how was Mexico?' Does Tom tell the truth? Does Angelina already know about Tom and Charlotte? In the scene try to build up as much tension as possible as Tom confronts his dilemma.

3. Tom seems to be at an age where he is easily embarrassed, and Tom and Dawn's parents seem to have forgotten that their children are growing up. Read through the script looking for moments where Tom is embarrassed by his parents.

   Create a video 'parenting manual' to be presented to Colin and Margery, advising them how best to reduce embarrassing moments. Show incidents from the play, and then their 'remedy' in the form of play, freeze and rewind sequences.

4. The family have been coming back to the same seaside resort for 'over twelve years'. As a sequence of still images with narrated captions, create the family's holiday photograph album in which they have pasted their favourite snaps from each holiday. Why do you think they choose to come back year after year?

Performing the play

1. The play uses a 'cross-cutting' technique where action moves swiftly between two stage locations. In groups, rehearse and perform the scene after Charlotte enters (pages 14-21), with Tom and Charlotte on one side of the stage and his parents and sister on the other. Why is this technique effective? Try to bring out the comic potential, as the two separate conversations are played in parallel. What are the main difficulties in rehearsing this part of the play, and how do you overcome them?

MEXICO

2. At a number of points the stage directions call for a strong wind, which blows the characters and props around. How can you suggest this on stage? Find the moments in the play, and stage them as effectively as you can.

3. Towards the end of the play Tom's father, Colin, finally starts to relax and enjoy himself. Read through the play and identify key moments where Colin's attitude starts to change. Perform a series of these moments, freezing the action at key points to allow Colin to speak his secret thoughts – his subtext – directly to the audience.

Writing

1. By the end of the play Colin and Margery seem to have found contentment. What has brought this about? What advice would you give the actors playing Colin and Margery? Write your advice in the form of director's notes for a production of the play.

2. Most of us take the idea of going on holiday for granted, but mass tourism is a relatively recent phenomenon. When did working people in the UK start taking annual holidays? Using libraries and the Internet, research the history of the British seaside resort. Present your findings as a short written history, or give a talk in front of the class.

The Corridor

Characters

Gayle	A school student in her mid-teens
Joanne	A school student in her mid-teens
Kenny	A young soldier from the First World War

The play is set in a bedroom of a hostel in Belgium in the present day. The room has two beds, two doors and a window. There is a mirror on the wall.

Early evening. **Joanne** is lying on her bed, reading. **Gayle**, barefoot, is holding one of the doors ajar and peering uncertainly into the gloom.

Gayle It's not a bathroom. Some sort of corridor, I think.

Joanne is absorbed in her book, and does not look up.

Joanne Really?

Gayle [Feeling for a light switch] It's weird. There's no light at all. It just – sort of – disappears into darkness.

There is a faint rumble from far down the corridor.

Did you hear that?

Joanne continues reading, answering Gayle without ever looking up.

Joanne Pipes. The whole hostel's creaky.

Gayle You have a look.

Joanne Where's it go?

Gayle I don't know.

Joanne It's probably blocked off.

Gayle	[*Uncertain*] Yeah. [*Closing the door*] So I can't wash my feet in there.
Joanne	Use the bathroom downstairs.
Gayle	[*Hobbling to her bed*] I can't walk that far.
Joanne	Ssh!
Gayle	If you'd told me before we came...

Joanne *sighs and stops reading.*

	If you'd told me what it was going to be like, I'd never have come.
Joanne	I'm trying to read.
Gayle	[*Massaging her foot*] Oww! Stuck in a minibus half the time…
Joanne	[*Ignoring her*] You know this place? Ypres?
Gayle	…Walking your legs off the rest.
Joanne	It's the first place they ever used poison gas.
Gayle	I don't want to know. What sort of holiday do you call this?
Joanne	[*Putting her book down in exasperation*] It's not a holiday!
Gayle	I know. I just said.
Joanne	It's a history trip. [*Sarcastically*] You know, to help with our coursework on World War One?
Gayle	I don't need telling. We spent all afternoon following old man Murray across a battlefield. What a let-down.
Joanne	I thought it was interesting.
Gayle	How would you know? You never lifted your head from the worksheets. Empty fields. Rows of white crosses. Where's the fun in that?
Joanne	It's not supposed to be fun. Ten thousand soldiers were killed by gas here.
Gayle	Enough! I've had it up to here [*indicating above head level*] without you starting.

THE CORRIDOR

Joanne *goes back to her book.* **Gayle** *starts putting on make-up.*

If you're so keen on Murray, why aren't you downstairs with him and the rest now?

Joanne	Games night is voluntary.
Gayle	It'd do you good to do something lively for once.
Joanne	Why don't you go, then?
Gayle	Quizzes? Balloon tennis? I don't think so.

Gayle *gets up to look at herself in the mirror and winces.*

I may never walk again.

Joanne	[Murmuring] It's a pity your mouth's not hurting an' all.
Gayle	I thought it'd be all right, a trip to Belgium. Bit of history during the day. Bars at night. Meet a few foreign lads. I like foreign lads. Don't you?
Joanne	Shushh!
Gayle	I nearly went out with a German last summer. He was over, learning English. I met him in the shop. Dieter he was called. Gorgeous.

She sits back on her bed and starts massaging her foot.

But have we seen a lad here? They're all six foot under and have been for ninety years. Mam thought I was mad, working Saturdays to pay for this. She'll kill herself when I go back. 'See anything nice Gayle?' – Yeah. Lots of lovely graveyards. –'Ooh. Smashing.'

Joanne	You looked a right idiot this afternoon.
Gayle	I couldn't help it.
Joanne	Trust you to go tumbling through the crosses.
Gayle	I tripped.
Joanne	You should've seen your face when you landed on a grave.

THE CORRIDOR

Gayle   Closest I've been to a lad all week. He had a nice name, mind. Kenny Walker. I almost went out with a Kenny once. Till he called round and caught sight of Nan.

Joanne   You'd've been all right if you were wearing proper boots like the rest of us.

Gayle   How was I supposed to know I'd need great clunky things like yours?

Joanne   It said so on the course info sheets.

Gayle   Oh, I didn't read all that rubbish. I knew what to expect. I just didn't expect so much of it, that's all.

Joanne picks up her book.

Don't start reading again. I'm fed up. Talk to me.

Joanne   Go downstairs if you want company.

Gayle   I haven't come to play silly games. We're away from home, Joanne. I don't have to listen to Mam moaning or wipe Nan's chin, for four whole days. I want to explore. Meet some new people.

Joanne   Well, go for a walk.

Gayle   Come with me. Murray won't let us out on our own, but two of us…

Joanne   [*Indicating her book*] I'm busy.

Gayle   What's the point of you coming here? You might have as well have locked yourself in a library.

Bored, she stretches out on the bed, then sits up trying to touch her toes. Joanne continues to read. There is a knocking sound. The girls glance up at the main bedroom door.

Hey, maybe room service has sent a couple of lads up.

Joanne   Answer it, then.

Gayle   You go. My feet.

Reluctantly Joanne gets up and opens the door. There's no one there. She closes it.

Joanne   Weird.

27

THE CORRIDOR

Gayle   It's the kids from the other school messing round, I bet. Have you seen them?

Joanne   One or two.

Gayle   About as fanciable as a box of badgers.

Joanne   If you say so.

*She lies back on her bed and resumes reading. **Gayle** finds a pair of high-fashion shoes and very gingerly puts one on.*

Gayle   [Wincing] Go on. Half an hour, that's all?

***Gayle** agonisingly puts the other shoe on and stands up.*

Joanne   I thought you were in agony.

Gayle   My feet are killing me. But sometimes you have to make sacrifices. There's a bar at the end of the road.

Joanne   I've told you. I'm busy.

Gayle   No one ever died wishing they'd stayed in more. One dance. A couple of drinks. We'll pass for old enough.

Joanne   I want to read about where we're going tomorrow.

Gayle   The Somme? Oh, it isn't flippin' natural, a lass being this interested in war.

*She sits down and takes her shoes off again. **Joanne** resumes reading. There is more knocking.*

That's the door again.

Joanne   You get it this time.

Gayle   What about my feet?

Joanne   Best take them with you.

*More knocking. **Gayle** stands up and hobbles towards the door.*

Gayle   If it's the other lot messing around…

*As **Gayle** is about to open the door, there is more knocking. **Joanne** sits up, puzzled.*

Joanne   [Indicating the other door] Gayle. This one.

Gayle	Oh. [*Hobbling over to it*] Must lead somewhere, after all.
	Gayle *opens the door.* **Kenny** *walks straight into the room, leaving the door open. He's dressed in old-fashioned baggy green trousers and wears braces over a white vest.*
Kenny	About time, too.
Gayle	Excuse me!
Kenny	[*Speaking slowly and deliberately.*] Have you – avez-vous – anything for a headache?
Gayle	Headache?
Kenny	Oui – mal de tête – savvy?
Gayle	What are you jabbering at us in French for?
Joanne	[*Barely looking up from her book*] And who said you could come in?
Kenny	[*Puzzled*] You're English?
Gayle	'Course we are.
Joanne	If you've got a headache go and see your teacher.
	Kenny *winces and puts his hands to his head.*
Gayle	Are you all right?
Kenny	Yes. I'm fine.
	He puts both hands to his head and groans.
Gayle	Sit down a minute.
	Gently she guides **Kenny** *down to sit on the edge of her bed.* **Joanne** *puts her book down in exasperation.*
Joanne	I'll go and get Mr Murray.
Kenny	[*Quickly*] No, don't get anyone.
Joanne	If you're ill…
Kenny	No… I'll be all right in a minute.
Gayle	Are you sure?

Kenny	Yes. It's just – something that happens – from time to time. [*Looking around with growing realization*] And it's started again.
Gayle	Like – a sort of seizure? My nan has those.
Kenny	It's strange. I get dizzy and can't breathe. I feel like I'm going to pass out and suddenly I don't know where I am any more.
Gayle	The bad news is you're in the most boring hostel in the whole of Belgium.
Kenny	[*Recovering*] It's all right. I'm coming round now. [*He sighs*] Oh, yeah. I know where I am and what I'm doing here.
Joanne	What brings your dizzy spells on?
Kenny	It's when I've been disturbed. A sudden noise. Someone bumping into you. That kind of thing.
Gayle	It'll be the games night downstairs.
Kenny	No. It was one of you two, I think. Clattering around.
	He gets up carefully and looks around the room.
Gayle	Hardly! We've been quiet as mice. [*Seeing an opportunity*] Though we're thinking of going to a bar, if you want to tag along.
Joanne	[*Under her breath*] Gayle, he's poorly!
Gayle	[*Under her breath*] He's a lad. Just about. [*To **Kenny***] How old are you?
Kenny	[*Quickly*] Seventeen.
Joanne	My brother looks older than you and he's only fourteen.
Kenny	I look young for my age, that's all. I'm old enough.
Gayle	What's your name?
Kenny	Everyone calls me Lucky. 'Cos I always pick the winner at dogs. [*Cheerily, now fully recovered*] Now I'd better find out about you two. What's your names?
Gayle	I'm Gayle. And my friend with no dress sense is Joanne.
Kenny	Pleased to meet you.

THE CORRIDOR

Gayle	Are you any good at dancing, Lucky?
Kenny	[*Ignoring the question*] Nice billet, this.
Joanne	[*Puzzled*] Billet?
Kenny	Room. Gaff. Much better than where I'm staying.
Joanne	Is it?
Kenny	Yeah. You wouldn't believe how dark and cold it is there.
Gayle	Well, ask to move, you idiot.
Kenny	You get used to it. Though it's nice to get out once in a while. What are you doing here?
Gayle	Same as you, I guess. School trip.
Kenny	[*Intrigued*] You're here to learn something?
Joanne	Yeah, for our exams. What about you?
Kenny	I suppose I came... for an adventure.
Gayle	Me, too. Only it's been nothing but flaming battlefields since we got here. If I see one more piece of barbed wire, I'll scream.
Kenny	I know exactly how you feel.
Joanne	Have you seen a lot of battlefields?
Kenny	Just the one.
Gayle	[*Pleading*] What about going to the bar with us? You can bring some of your friends.
Kenny	Some other time, maybe.
	Gayle sinks back onto her bed.
Gayle	[*Sarcastically*] Great!
Kenny	What have you learned so far?
Joanne	Loads.

31

THE CORRIDOR

Gayle	Nothing worth knowing.
Kenny	Nothing at all?
Gayle	It's morbid, bothering about World War One. They ought to concrete all the museums and graveyards over. Build something useful.
Joanne	Gayle!
Kenny	She's entitled to her opinion.
Gayle	Thank you. [*To* **Kenny**] Go on, just a couple of drinks.
Kenny	Sorry.
Gayle	You're as boring as she is.
Kenny	You reckon it should all be forgotten?
Gayle	Why not? Instead of filling people's heads full of war, till they just want to do it all over again. Get some use out of it, I say.
Kenny	And what do you think, Joanne?
Joanne	It's got a use. To remind everyone how terrible war is, so it doesn't happen again.
Gayle	But it keeps on happening. World War Two, Vietnam, the Falklands, Iraq. [*Glancing at* **Joanne**] See? She thinks I don't know any history, but I do.
Kenny	Then maybe there isn't any point reminding people about the bloodshed here.
Gayle	Exactly. Forget about it.
Joanne	No! If more people understood what the First World War was really like, they wouldn't be so quick to start fighting again.
Kenny	What was it like?
Joanne	I don't know.
Gayle	Yes she does. It's all she ever bloody reads about.
Kenny	Is that right?

32

Joanne	I'm doing an assignment on life in the trenches, so I have been reading a bit.
Kenny	Go on, then. Tell me about it.
Joanne	It must have been awful. All mud, blood and lice.

Kenny *scratches himself absent-mindedly.*

Shells and bullets flying over your head all the time. It was so bad, the ones who got home never liked to talk about it.

Gayle	Our teacher goes on about the rats. Said they were everywhere. Eurrgh!
Kenny	Too bloody true. Always trying to get into the potted meat… [Quickly] So I'm told. [To **Joanne**] Carry on.
Joanne	The worst thing must have been waiting for the order to climb out of your trench and run towards the enemy guns. If you did, you'd most likely get killed. If you refused – if your nerve had gone – your own officers shot you.
Kenny	[Impressed] You know a lot.
Gayle	It's all she does know. She's a history freak.
Joanne	I think it's interesting to read about.
Kenny	It must be. Though words in a book can't tell you what it actually felt like.
Joanne	Well, no one knows that now.
Kenny	[Amused] Don't they?
Joanne	They're all dead.
Kenny	Oh, yeah. Of course they are. [Short pause] There was one thing I always wanted to know about life in the trenches, Joanne.
Joanne	What's that?
Kenny	What do you reckon they were like at night?
Gayle	Flippin' 'eck! Don't get her started.
Joanne	Horrible, I expect. Some of the officers had little rooms dug in the earth, but most of the men slept where they fought. When the rains came, some of them even drowned in the mud.

THE CORRIDOR

Kenny   Is that so?

Joanne   [*Growing animated*] And after a battle, the survivors had to listen to the wounded moaning in no-man's-land all through the night. Sometimes they even had to keep dead bodies in the trenches, because it was too dangerous to climb out and bury them. So the corpses got stacked like sandbags...

Gayle   [*Disgusted*] Joanne!

Joanne   ...only, the rotting flesh attracted even more rats.

Gayle   Will you shut up!

Kenny   It's nice to meet someone who knows something for a change.

Joanne   I don't know a lot.

Kenny   I'd always wondered about the nights. Didn't miss much, did I?

Gayle   [*Looking at **Kenny** as though he's mad*] Eh?

Joanne   [*More thoughtful*] What do you mean?

Kenny   'Wipers' we called this place. Didn't know much French.

Joanne   You mean Ypres?

Kenny   You see, I'd taken it personal when Kitchener pointed his finger and said, 'Your country needs YOU.' So I answered the poster and signed up, along with a few of my mates from the Mile End Road.

Gayle   [*Disbelieving*] What?

Kenny   Proud to serve King and Country in the war to end all wars. Kissed my sweetheart goodbye at the tram station. Amy. Nice girl. Butcher's daughter. And there I was, happy as Larry, buffing my boots for the parade ground. Left! Right! Left! Right! Yes, sir! No, sir! Playing at soldiers, like we did when we were kids.

Gayle   [*To **Joanne**, under her breath*] He's out of his mind.

Joanne   Sssh!

                *During **Kenny**'s next speech, the lighting in the room changes, and sound effects of trench warfare echo down the corridor.*

34

Kenny	Then the call came. The Boche had broken through at Hill 60. We had to throw in everything to drive them back. Even raw recruits like me. By the time I got there, the battle had been going backwards and forwards for ages. *[With wry amusement]* All that fuss over one filthy little heap of mud. *[Short pause]* Of course, me and my mates had heard about chlorine gas by then, but we didn't really know what to expect. First day in the dugouts, they chucked it at us from howitzers. We weren't ready. Didn't have no masks on, or anything. This cloud of greenish yellow mist rolled all along the line towards us. Soon as it hit, it stung your eyes, like someone slashing them with a razor. Then you started coughing up, till you felt you were going to spew your guts out. – *[To **Joanne**]* They can't explain that feeling in a book. I pulled out a hanky – one Amy gave me specially when she saw me off. She'd stitched a heart on it. I spat and clapped it over my face. Didn't do no good. In no time my mouth was full of snot and slime. All of us were choking, still sucking in the yellow poison, till you couldn't see nothing at all. That's when I panicked. I was desperate to climb out. I dug my nails into something slippery and wet and tried to scramble over it. Maybe it was a sandbag. I didn't care then. I felt like I had flames bursting out of my chest. I had to run, only I slipped and fell back. Then there were others scrambling over me. Kicking and choking. Trampling on me to get out, themselves. They didn't mean no harm. I'd've done the same, only I didn't have the strength no more. One big retch and then there was nothing. Sort of a dizzy blackness, that's all. And then the pain stopped.

The sound effects fade and the light reverts to normal. **Kenny** *comes out of his reverie.*

That's good. My head's cleared now. It always does when someone listens.

Joanne	*[Quietly]* What's your real name?
Kenny	Didn't I say? I'm Kenny. Kenny Walker.
Gayle	*[Disbelieving]* What?
Kenny	I won't take up any more of your time, girls.
Gayle	Kenny Walker?
Kenny	That's me. You won't find me in any book. But I'm real, all right.

He goes back to the door he came in by.

THE CORRIDOR

Gayle   Hold on!

Kenny   Don't worry. You'll forget me quick enough. People always seem to. But if anything I've said sticks, my death won't have been a complete waste, will it? Ta-ta now.

He goes out, closing the door behind him. Pause.

Gayle   *[Shaken]* It's a wind-up. It's a bloody wind-up!

Joanne   Is it?

Gayle   It's bloody Mr Murray set this up. Just because we didn't join in games night!

Joanne   I don't think so, Gayle. He was real.

Gayle   He can't have been. *[Pause]* He was way too young for a soldier.

*She goes slowly over to the door **Kenny** left by.*

Joanne   I read about lads like him, lying about their age to join the army. *[Picking up her book]* Where was it?

*[She lies back, leafing through the pages. **Gayle** opens the door and looks into the darkness]*

Gayle   It's not a bathroom. Some sort of corridor, I think.

Joanne   *[Without looking up]* Really?

Gayle   *[Feeling for a light switch]* It's weird. There's no light at all. It just – sort of – disappears into darkness.

There is a faint rumble from far down the corridor.

Did you hear that?

Joanne   Pipes. The whole hostel's creaky.

Gayle   You have a look.

Joanne   Where's it go?

Gayle   I don't know.

Joanne   It's probably blocked off.

Gayle   *[Uncertain]* Yeah. *[Closing the door]* So I can't wash my feet in there.

Joanne	Use the bathroom downstairs.
	Pause.
Gayle	If I do, will you come out with me afterwards?
Joanne	[*Lowering her book*] Where?
Gayle	[*Going to look out of the window*] There's a bit of a moon. You'll think I'm daft, but I fancy another look at the graveyard.
Joanne	What for?
Gayle	I don't know. I feel sorry for all those young lads, that's all.
	Joanne *sits up.*
Joanne	Go on, then.
	Blackout.

THE CORRIDOR

World War I changed the way people thought about modern warfare. Many British soldiers signing up to fight in 1914 believed the war would be 'over by Christmas'. It was not until four years of bitter fighting had left an estimated 10 million dead, that an armistice was signed and a brief peace settled over Europe.

Group activities

How much do you know about World War I? In small groups, discuss what you understand by terms such as 'shell shock', 'Pals battalions', 'mustard gas', 'over the top' or 'trench warfare'? Do you know any other words or phrases that came out of the Great War?

1. In your groups, read some poems by World War I poets such as Wilfred Owen or Siegfried Sassoon. Write a list of memorable words, phrases or metaphors from the poems. Create a series of five still images inspired by what you have read. Have one member of your group narrate from the poems, as the rest of you hold each image for a few seconds before changing to the next.

2. Read the section where Kenny tells the girls about leaving his girlfriend Amy at the tram station. Imagine what this event might have been like. At the start of the war, in a bid to maintain morale and to encourage recruitment, soldiers from the same family, town, street or district were often put into the same unit. These became known as 'Pals battalions'. Kenny would be among hundreds or even thousands of soldiers leaving to fight in the Great War.

   In your group, choose someone to 'hot-seat' the role of Amy. Start the exercise by asking how Amy feels about her sweetheart going off to war. Is she proud of him? Is she worried that Kenny might never come back? Now change the actor playing Amy. This time the hot-seating takes place soon after Amy has found out that Kenny has been gassed at Ypres. What are her feelings now?

3. Use some of the images and ideas from the hot-seating exercise to create two improvised scenes: Kenny saying goodbye to Amy at the tram station, Amy receiving the news of Kenny's death.

   Once you have created both scenes, devise a way to merge the scenes by cutting from one to the other. You might decide to split the performance space into two halves and have actors playing more than one role. Where you decide to cut between the scenes is important; try to choose moments that contrast significantly, to highlight the different mood and atmosphere of the scenes.

THE CORRIDOR

4. Read the speech in which Kenny describes being gassed at Ypres. Who do you think this speech is directed at? What do Gayle and Joanne do while he is talking? What sound effects do you think might support Kenny's description? Experiment with different ways of saying the speech. For instance, try reading it in a measured and calm way, then in a way that reflects the panic and fear that Kenny must have felt. Which way communicates this terrible event most effectively? Working in your group, create a series of stylised movements and gestures to accompany the speech. Introduce sounds or words that could be whispered, chanted or sung in the background.

Performing the play

1. Joanne and Gayle have very different attitudes towards history and the school trip they are on. In pairs, read from the beginning of the play to the point where they hear the first knocking sound (page 27). Think about how you can show the characters' contrasting attitudes in performance.

   Choose a short section from the first few pages to focus on. Experiment with different ways of interpreting the stage directions, for example: Gayle is preoccupied with her sore feet, Joanne the book. How can you use your voice and body language to show the two characters becoming increasingly frustrated with each other?

2. Using the same section of text, identify two moments where the action can freeze. With the action frozen, each character delivers a short speech directly to the audience, describing their feelings about their friend, the war or the school trip so far. This exercise is sometimes called 'step-out'. When you say your lines to the audience, remember you are still in character, and this should be reflected in your voice, facial expression, body language and gestures.

Writing

Many of the soldiers who volunteered to fight in the early months of the First World War did so out of a sense of patriotic duty, and, as Kenny says, for 'an adventure'. Imagine what it must have felt like to arrive at the front and experience the horror of trench warfare first-hand.

Write a letter from Kenny, to Amy or to his parents. He has just arrived at Ypres, or 'Wipers' as it was nicknamed by the British soldiers. Use the script to find descriptions of life in the trenches – the rats, the sounds of dead or dying men, the mud. Remember that Kenny might not want the people back home to worry about him; how might this affect how he writes the letter?

39

Goodnight, Night owl

Characters

Johnny	A local radio late-night DJ
Frank	A lorry driver, engaged to be married for the second time
Margaret	His ex-wife
Ali	Their daughter, aged 15
Karen	Frank's fiancée, in her late 20s, works in a motorway service station

The play is set in a radio studio, a service station, the cab of a heavy-goods vehicle (HGV) and two adjacent bedrooms in Margaret and Ali's house. It's the middle of the night. The action of the play cuts fluidly between the different locations, and lighting can be used to pick out the actors as required.

The tracks played by Johnny Morgan should help create the right atmosphere for the play. You might wish to research and make your own choice of music. Otherwise, here are just a few suggestions: 'In the still of the night' by The Five Satins could be Johnny's first record; Ali's dilemma could be highlighted by 'Should I stay or should I go?' by The Clash; Margaret might recall the break-up over her marriage to the sound of 'Heard it through the grapevine' by Marvin Gaye.

SCENE 1

The radio studio. **Johnny**, *wearing headphones, fades out the last bars of a music track.*

Johnny   [Into mic] Welcome to the Johnny Morgan show. I'm going to be with you through the long dark stretches of the night, when hearts open and tales get told. Tonight we're discussing 'Second Time Around – Do second marriages work?' What do you think? Have you had experience of breaking up and trying again? Or been part of a family where that's happened? Why not share what you've been through with us? You're only a text, an e-mail or a phone call away, so please, get in touch now. I want to know what's on your mind.

40

SCENE 2

The cab of **Frank**'s HGV.

Frank   [*As if to the driver in front*] Bloody caravans! It's the middle of the night, mate! You want to be at home, not crawling along a single carriageway at fifty miles an hour. I've milk in the back of this, you know. It'll be cheese by the time I get there.

His hands-free mobile phone rings. He presses a button on the dashboard.

Hello?

Lights up on **Karen**, sitting in her catering uniform at a table in the service station where she works.

Karen   [*Into her mobile phone*] Frank?

Frank   All right, love? Are you busy?

Karen   No, I'm on my break. It's quiet. A couple of truckies and a minibus, that's all. Where are you?

Frank   About two miles short of the motorway. Stuck behind the slowest driver in the whole of Great Britain.

Karen   Never mind. How long before you get here?

Frank   A good while yet, I'm afraid.

Karen   [*Disappointed*] Ahh.

Frank   And I'll want a full English when I do.

Karen   You're having scrambled eggs, and no butter.

Frank   [*Not happy*] Karen…

Karen   You want to be able to get into your suit on Saturday, don't you?

Frank   [*Wryly*] Is this what my life's going to be like from now on?

Karen   Yeah. Any complaints?

Frank   None at all.

GOODNIGHT, NIGHT OWL

Karen   Listen, sweetheart. I've got to start again in a minute, but I wanted to be sure you've got your radio on.

Frank   What time is it? [*Checking the clock on his dashboard*] Oh 'eck, I've missed the start.

Karen   Well, listen carefully to the rest.

Frank switches on his radio. Music plays softly under their conversation.

Frank   What for?

Karen   Just listen. Now I've got to go. See you soon, sweetheart.

Frank   Bye, love.

Karen switches off her mobile and goes to the counter. The lights fade out on the cab of the HGV and the service station. The music builds slightly as lights fade up on Ali's bedroom, where Ali is typing something into her computer.

SCENE 3

There's a knock at Ali's bedroom door. She hurriedly finishes typing and clicks to send an e-mail.

Ali   Come in.

Margaret comes into the room.

Margaret   I thought you'd be asleep by now. Then I heard the music.

Ali   Is it too loud, Mum?

She turns the music down on her computer.

Margaret   No. I'm going to listen myself, while I take my make-up off. But isn't it a bit old-fogeyish for you?

Ali   It's all right.

Pause.

Margaret   Is it because your dad liked this station?

Ali   You do an' all, don't you?

Margaret   I think Johnny Morgan's good.

42

GOODNIGHT, NIGHT OWL

Ali   So do I.

Margaret   That's all right, then. [*Feeling awkward*] As long as there's nothing keeping you
               awake?

Ali   [*Indicating her computer*] I'm trying to get the cards out, that's all.

Margaret   You and your silly games. Good job it's not term time.

Ali   I'll get my head down soon.

Margaret   Good. [*Pause*] You're sure you're not worrying about anything?

Ali   No. Not at all.

Margaret   Sleep well, then.

               She starts to move away.

Ali   You too.

Margaret   [*Stopping at the door*] Oh, I meant to say, Ali, I was having a little think earlier...

Ali   Yeah?

Margaret   You know the new shopping mall in town?

Ali   By the station? It's meant to be great.

Margaret   Well, you and me both need something new for summer, so how about a trip
               there some time soon?

Ali   Definitely. It's got a good art shop as well.

Margaret   We'll have to have a look, then. [*Casually*] I was wondering about going at the
               weekend.

Ali   [*Trying to mask her disappointment*] Oh.

Margaret   Maybe Saturday? If you're free.

Ali   Er... I'm not quite sure what's happening then.

Margaret   Oh? Still making your mind up?

Ali   [*Awkwardly*] Can I tell you tomorrow?

GOODNIGHT, NIGHT OWL

Margaret   Of course. [*Blowing a kiss*] Now, don't stay up too late.

She leaves the room.

Ali   'Night.

When her mother has closed the door, she sighs. The action shifts back to **Johnny** *in the radio studio, who now fades out the music on his mixing desk.*

SCENE 4

Johnny   [*Into mic*] Plenty of messages have been coming in about second marriages. Some people saying it's the best thing that's ever happened to them. [*Reading from a computer screen*] 'Why stay in a loveless relationship? Everybody suffers then, especially the children.' One or two callers aren't so sure. [*Reading from the screen*] 'Couples give up without even trying to make a marriage work these days. Then they're surprised when the next one doesn't turn out like a fairytale either.' And I've had an intriguing email from someone simply called 'Night Owl'. Night Owl's got a really important decision to make about a second wedding, but he or she's not sure what to do. Whatever course of action they take, someone Night Owl loves is going to be badly hurt. Maybe if you told us a little more about your situation, Night Owl, we'd be able to help. So please, get back in touch. And, in the meantime, let the music take some of the load.

Johnny fades in another music track, as the action returns to **Frank** *in the cab of his HGV. He is pressing keys on his dashboard mobile phone as he drives. Across the stage, lights fade back up on* **Ali** *in her bedroom. Her mobile phone rings. She checks the caller's name and answers.*

SCENE 5

Ali   [*Into phone*] Dad?

Frank   How are you doing, Ali-Pally?

Ali   Fine. I'm great.

Frank   Sorry to call so late.

Ali   It's all right. I'm playing cards on my computer.

Frank   I thought you would be. And I didn't want to leave it any longer.

Ali	Leave what?
Frank	Getting in touch. I've not heard from you in days.
Ali	Sorry. I've been busy.
Frank	It's all right. I'm not chasing you up. I just wondered if you'd decided yet.
Ali	About Saturday?
Frank	Yes.
Ali	Erm... I'm still not quite sure.
Frank	[Disappointed] It doesn't matter.
Ali	I'm thinking about it.
Frank	How's your mother?
Ali	All right.
Frank	Not being awkward?
Ali	[Quickly] No.
Frank	I don't want to make this hard for you, Ali, but... well, me and Karen... you know it'd mean a lot to us...
Ali	[Cutting him off] Yeah, I do. That's why I'm thinking about it.
Frank	All right, darling. Do whatever you think's best.
Ali	I'm trying to.
Frank	Just remember, if me and Karen move away afterwards – and we're thinking about it – it might not be so easy to see you in future. So Saturday would be really special.
Ali	Yeah. I'll tell you tomorrow.
Frank	I'm coming to an awkward interchange, so I'll say goodbye. Love you, Ali.
Ali	Love you, Dad.
Frank	And Karen sends her love too.

GOODNIGHT, NIGHT OWL

Ali doesn't say anything. **Frank** *switches off his dashboard mobile, as the lights fade out on the HGV and* **Ali**'s *bedroom.*

SCENE 6

Lights up on **Margaret**'s *bedroom and the radio studio.* **Margaret** *is sitting in front of a dressing-table mirror, writing a text message on her mobile. She reads it through, and sends. She seems much more anxious than when she was speaking to* **Ali**. *In the radio studio* **Johnny** *fades out the music.*

Johnny   [Into mic] Thank you all for contacting me. The airwaves are buzzing with stories. Some are happy. But there's a lot of heartbreak out there too. A text has just been patched through. [Looking at screen] From 'M'.

Margaret sits up to take notice — this is her text.

M says second marriages are all very well, but what about the people who get left behind? Her text reads, 'I'm the idiot of a first wife, who didn't realize that my husband was seeing someone else...

Margaret   [To the radio] ...until it was too late. Doesn't make you feel too good, when you've put years into a marriage, only for him to announce he doesn't love you any more; that he's moving in with someone else.

Johnny   [Into mic] And there's a lot more besides. Clearly M is a woman in pain. What really got through to me was this. [Reading from the screen] 'I can bear losing my marriage but I can't bear him...

Margaret   [To the radio] ...taking my daughter as well. Sometimes I think she's all I've got left. My looks are going fast. My hope's disappeared. But I've still got a wonderful girl who loves me and has stuck by me through all of this. I don't mind her seeing her father; that's only natural. But I won't have this other woman — the one who smashed up our home — come creeping round my daughter, trying to be her best friend and take my place. I won't have it!

Johnny   [Turning away from the screen] Thank you, M.

Lights down on **Margaret**'s *bedroom.*

Now I've a caller on line one. Karen, I believe?

He presses a button on the control panel. Lights up on the service station, where **Karen** *is standing by the counter, using her mobile.*

GOODNIGHT, NIGHT OWL

	Hello, Karen.
Karen	[Into mobile] Hello, Johnny. I'll have to be quick. I'm working.
Johnny	Where?
Karen	At an all-night services. We're playing you loud and clear, all through the restaurant.
Johnny	What's on your mind, Karen?
Karen	We'll be busy soon, so I wanted to ask you to play a request for me, Johnny.
Johnny	What do you want to hear?
Karen	Anything romantic. You see, I'm getting married on Saturday.
Johnny	Congratulations.
Karen	It's the second chance for both of us. Only this time it's going to work out. I know it is.
Johnny	Let's hope so.
Karen	It will, because I'm marrying the most wonderful man in the world. And I know he's listening, so Frank, I love you. And I know you're worried about Saturday, but you don't have to be.
Johnny	What's Frank worrying about?
Karen	Something that means a lot to him. That's all he'd want me to say.
Johnny	Okay.
Karen	It'll turn out all right, you'll see, Frank – Thanks, Johnny.
Johnny	Thank you, Karen. This next song's for you and Frank. And let's hope that whatever's worrying him about your wedding day is soon sorted out.

Johnny brings in another music track, as the lights fade out on the studio and the service station.

SCENE 7

Ali's bedroom. She is typing. There is an urgent knocking at the door. Ali quickly clicks with the mouse to send an e-mail, then clicks to change screen, as the door opens.

GOODNIGHT, NIGHT OWL

Margaret [*Furious*] Do you know who that was? Did you hear her?

Ali Just now?

Margaret How dare she!

Ali Calm down, Mum.

Margaret She's marrying him on Saturday; she's got what she wanted. Isn't that enough? Does she have to flaunt it in my face? Tell the whole county what she's done?

Ali I'm sure she didn't mean it like that.

Margaret You wouldn't know, Ali. You don't know how sneaking and conniving that woman's been. Your father let slip he'd been using those services for a year before anything started. She'd been planning it all that time.

Ali You don't know that, Mum.

Margaret Why are you sticking up for her?

Ali I'm not.

Margaret Do you like her, an' all?

Ali No. I don't know. I don't know her.

Margaret [*Close to tears*] Oh, I'm sorry, love – I know it's not fair.

Ali gets up and puts her arm round her mother.

Ali It's all right. I don't mind.

Margaret If there was anyone else to talk to. I don't want to drag you into things between me and your father. It's not right. You're too young to understand.

Ali I'm not. I'm fine.

Margaret I've been managing all right. I'm used to doing without him now. Wouldn't want him back. But to hear her – going on about getting wed this weekend. As though Frank and me never meant anything.

She is now crying.

Ali It's okay, Mum. It's okay.

48

Margaret [*Regaining her composure*] I don't mind them getting married. But inviting you – you know what that's about?

Ali Dad wants me there, that's all.

Margaret She wants you there. To get to know you. To make you like her. First it was Frank. Now she wants to take you from me as well.

__Margaret__ puts a hand over her eyes. __Ali__ comforts her. Lights fade down on __Ali__'s bedroom and back up on the service station, where __Karen__ is preparing food behind the counter. __Frank__ enters.

SCENE 8

Frank All right, love?

Karen Hi. [*Quietly*] I'd kiss you, but the boss is around.

Frank And thanks.

Karen You heard?

Frank It was a lovely surprise. With you saying to listen, I thought you'd sent in a request. I didn't expect to hear your voice coming out of the speakers.

Karen I was so nervous. Go and sit down. I'll bring your breakfast over.

__Frank__ goes to sit at the table. __Karen__ comes out from behind the counter with a plate of scrambled eggs.

Frank You didn't sound nervous.

Karen My stomach was all scrunched up. This producer tells you when you're about to talk to Johnny. I didn't think any words were going to come out.

Frank You sounded great.

Karen I meant it, Frank. Not just that I love you. You know that. But what I said about things working out. That it'll be all right on Saturday.

Frank [*Trying to sound cheerful*] 'Course it will.

__Karen__ looks round to see if she's being watched by her boss, then sits down next to __Frank__.

Karen I know you've been worrying.

Frank That's only natural before a wedding, isn't it?

GOODNIGHT, NIGHT OWL

Karen	About Ali not coming.
Frank	[Smiling] You do know me well, don't you?
Karen	I think I'm starting to.
Frank	I rang her. She still hasn't made her mind up.
Karen	Oh.
Frank	It's Margaret who doesn't want her to come, of course.
Karen	Suppose… suppose the worst happened and she didn't make it? We'll see her plenty of times after we're married, won't we?
Frank	It isn't quite the same though, is it?
Karen	Well, no, but…
Frank	[Cutting her off] I've no regrets about leaving Margaret. But I feel guilty about Ali.
Karen	Why? You've been such a good dad.
Frank	Look what I've put her through. All the rows. The divorce. I'll never forget the way she looked at me, the day I walked out of the house for good.
Karen	Do you really think she'd've been better off if you'd stayed?
Frank	[Ruefully] No. There was always such an atmosphere. It must have made life awful for her.
Karen	That's why it's better you left.
	Pause.
Frank	I don't know why it all went so wrong with Margaret – the hours we worked, maybe. The way the years changed us. You can't stay childhood sweethearts for ever. You develop, you grow. We just grew in different ways. Wanted different things. It was over long before it was over.
Karen	I'd never have gone out with you, if I'd thought there was anything left in your marriage.
Frank	I know.

Karen	I know what it's like to be cheated on. I wouldn't do it to another woman. That's why I kept quiet for a whole year when you started coming here. Even though I thought you were great. I didn't want to do anything to break you and Margaret up.
Frank	You didn't, love. Things were already a mess between us before you and me got friendly.
Karen	And I wouldn't do anything to hurt things between you and Ali.
Frank	[Looking off] I think your boss is wondering where you've got to.
Karen	Oh, yes.

Karen gets up hurriedly and wipes an imaginary spot from the table.

	I'll play it any way you like, Frank. But I just think you should be prepared for Saturday. Not have your hopes too high.
Frank	It's silly, I know. But if Ali comes to the wedding, it'll be like – she doesn't hold a grudge for what I've done. She's forgiven me. And that would mean so much.

SCENE 9

The radio station. **Johnny** *fades down the music and looks at the screen.*

Johnny	[Into mic] Still your stories are pouring in. Night Owl has e-mailed again. She still hasn't given a name, but she's told me a little more about herself. She says she can't eat and she can't sleep; she's feeling torn apart worrying about what's going to happen at the weekend. That's all she says. She's worried sick. Please, Night Owl, pick up the phone and ring. You know my number by now.

Lights up on **Ali**'s *room, where* **Ali** *is sat holding her mobile and wondering whether to ring.*

It's your choice, of course. You can sit alone, feeling responsible for the whole world going wrong. Or you can talk...

Decisively, **Ali** *dials on her mobile.*

...and let some of the pain out. [Short pause] Ah, I've a light on line two.

He presses a button.

GOODNIGHT, NIGHT OWL

Hello?

Ali   [*Into mobile*] Hello? Johnny?

Johnny Hi.

Ali   It's me. Night Owl.

Johnny Good to hear from you. How are you feeling?

Ali   Rubbish. I've got a decision to make by tomorrow morning, and whatever I do is going to be wrong.

Johnny You said you were going to end up hurting somebody.

Ali   That's right. My mum or my dad.

*Lights up on **Margaret**'s bedroom and the service station. **Margaret** is taking her make-up off in front of the mirror. **Frank** is eating his breakfast and **Karen** is wiping the counter. Gradually they stop what they're doing and listen, as they realize who is talking.*

You see, my dad's getting married again. And he wants me to be at the ceremony. He says it's all right if I don't go, but I can tell from his voice he really wants me there.

Johnny But there's a problem?

Ali   I love him loads. I want him to be happy. But I love my mum just as much. She's been through an awful lot this last couple of years. She didn't want the divorce. She thought they could patch things up.

Johnny I see.

Ali   And Dad getting married again – it's cutting her up. Making her feel forgotten. Useless. She says it's up to me if I go or not. But when I think about going... I picture her on her own, trying to keep busy while the wedding's going on. All on her own. Like she's got no one. Like I betrayed her.

Johnny So you feel you have to choose between what your father wants and what your mother wants?

Ali   Yeah. I'm being torn both ways. Imagining how they'll feel if I don't do what they want. I love both of them. I can't choose.

52

GOOD NIGHT, NIGHT OWL

Johnny   Have you tried telling them this?

Ali   Yeah. Sort of.

Johnny   But it's not easy?

Ali   I can't stand the hurt in their voices when I try. So I end up saying what they want to hear. Or nothing at all. That's why I've phoned you. I hope they're listening. I want them to know how much I love them. And I always will. And because I do something for one of them, it doesn't mean I don't love the other one just as much. It doesn't mean that at all.

Johnny   Your heart's big enough for both of them?

Ali   Yeah… Yeah, that's it exactly.

Johnny   I hope they are listening, Night Owl. And remember, this situation is not of your making. All you can do is try to make your parents understand how you really feel. I know that'll take courage. Please stay in touch and let us know what you decide. And in the meantime, the next piece of music is dedicated to you.

Johnny fades in a new track. Lights go down on the studio and the service station. Ali thinks for a moment, then, taking her mobile with her, goes into her mother's room.

Ali   Mum, were you listening?

Margaret   [Quietly] Yes, love.

Ali   [Holding out her mobile] The number's on a preset. Just press two.

Margaret   What for? [Slowly realizing] Your want me to phone your father?

Ali   Things are how they are, Mum. Not how you'd like them to be. But one thing you don't ever have to worry about is losing me. It's not even possible. Like the man said, my heart's big enough for both of you.

Pause. Margaret, rather uncertainly, takes the mobile and presses a number on the keypad. Frank's mobile rings as lights come back up on the service station. Karen is back behind the counter. Frank, getting ready to leave, takes his mobile out and answers it.

Frank   Hello? Ali?

Margaret   No, it's not.

53

GOODNIGHT, NIGHT OWL

Frank   Margaret?

Margaret   Is she there now? Karen?

Frank   [Stunned] You want to talk to Karen?

Margaret   Yes.

Frank   [Hesitating] Why? You're not going to make trouble?

Margaret   Put her on, will you, Frank? It's taking everything I've got to make this call. Don't make me wait.

Frank   [Moving towards **Karen**] Karen, love. Is there any chance of you taking this? It's my ex-wife.

Karen   [Quietly] What?

              Frank shrugs and hands her the phone. She answers it nervously.

              Hello?

Margaret   Karen?

Karen   Yes.

Margaret   Maybe it's time we talked.

              *Lights down on **Margaret**'s bedroom and the service station, and back up on the studio, where **Johnny** fades out a piece of music.*

SCENE 10

Johnny   [Into mic] My show's almost over. Outside the dark is at its thickest and our imperfect, messy world is finally about to rest. I hope at least one of you out there will sleep better tonight. Your last e-mail tells me you've made your decision.

              *Lights up on **Ali**'s bedroom. **Ali** is sitting in front of the computer. **Margaret** is standing behind her.*

Margaret   No wonder our phone bill's rocketing, all the times you've been in touch with him tonight.

GOODNIGHT, NIGHT OWL

Ali   You're honestly okay about me going on Saturday?

Margaret   No. …At least not till we've been to the mall and bought you something decent to wear. I won't have you turn up scruffy at a wedding. That'd show me up.

Ali hugs her mother. Lights down on Ali's bedroom.

Johnny   To all of you listening, thank you for your company. Sleep well. And especially, our youngest caller this evening. Goodnight, Night Owl.

Blackout.

GOODNIGHT, NIGHT OWL

Group activities

1. On a sheet of blank paper draw outlines of the four characters in the play. As you read through the script, write down the key facts that you learn about the character inside their outline; outside the outline write things that you can guess, or infer, about the characters.

    Mount the four outlines on the wall to make a large square. Draw arrows and write phrases which link the characters, describing their relationships to each other and the feelings they have.

2. Devise a scene in which Ali first learns that there are problems in the relationship between her mother and father. Try to avoid being too obvious! Once you have created your scene, freeze the action at key moments and allow Ali to comment on the action. What insight does it give us into Ali's state of mind?

3. Ali's dilemma seems to be resolved when Margaret speaks to Karen on the telephone. How do the two women view each other at the beginning of the play, and how do their views change? In pairs, improvise the conversation which took place between them. Remember that it has taken a lot of courage for Margaret to ring Karen, and that the two of them have never spoken before.

4. Create, as a sequence of still pictures, wedding photographs of Ali, Frank and Karen. Use levels, facial expression and gesture to convey the relationships between the characters. Was it a perfectly happy day, or were there hidden tensions and anxieties? Although Margaret wasn't at the wedding, can you find a way of suggesting her 'presence' – or her absence – in one of the photographs?

5. Devise a scene taking place a year later, which includes all of the characters in the play. How have things changed? Are things any easier for Ali? How are relations between Margaret, Frank and Karen?

Performing the play

1.   *Goodnight, Night Owl* uses the technique of cross-cutting between different locations. Before staging the play, mark out the five acting areas in masking tape on the floor. Using labels, mark out the essential furniture and props in each of the locations. Think carefully about how you can give each area a distinctive character using a minimum of props. For example, how can you suggest the different qualities of Ali's and Margaret's bedrooms?

      Choose key moments from the play when the action moves from one location to another. Now place actors in each of the locations, and explore techniques that move the action fluently from one location to the next. Will you use freezes, or blackouts, or can you find an entirely original way of cross-cutting?

2.   Look through the script and find sections where music plays underneath the action (underscore). Starting with Adrian Flynn's suggestions on page 40, experiment using music of different styles to create the atmosphere you want for particular scenes. Perform the scenes in front of the other groups. Have they made similar choices? Which were most effective, and why?

Writing

Write a series of e-mails sent by 'Night Owl' – Ali – to Johnny, from the time that her parents' marriage began to break up to the day of Frank's wedding. Try to capture Ali's feelings as she starts to recognize what is happening to her and her family. How has her mood changed by the time of her final e-mail?

Siege

Characters

Hugh Brideoak	A battle-scarred royalist officer
Richard Brideoak	His elder son. A royalist officer
James Brideoak	The younger son. A parliamentarian soldier

The play is set in and just outside the stables of a besieged castle in 1644, the third year of the English Civil War. Although the setting and characters are fictional, they draw on real people and events; some elements in particular are drawn from the siege of Lathom House in Lancashire. The shabby state of Richard and Hugh's clothing and general demeanour should reflect the fact that they have been under siege for a number of weeks. James has disguised himself as a carter to gain access to the castle.

Sound effects – occasional, isolated musket shots and the shouting of orders, for example, may help suggest that the stables are part of a garrison under siege.

The stables, which are empty of horses. Richard is chasing an unseen rat with his sword.

Richard Hold your ground! You're for the pot, you foul little…

He changes direction to follow the rat, strikes at it, then gives up, bleakly amused.

Well run, Sir Rat. Essex himself must have trained you to flee so quickly.

*He sits on a small hay bale, and resumes the interrupted activity of sharpening his sword. There are other swords propped against the side of the bale. His father, **Hugh**, comes furtively onstage with **James**, who carries a wooden staff and wears a woollen cap pulled low on his head. **Hugh** stops outside the entrance of the stables.*

Hugh Stay here a moment. It will be a shock – a joyful shock. But your brother must be prepared.

James Quickly then, father. Before I'm seen.

***Hugh** goes into the stables.*

Hugh	We have a visitor, Richard.
Richard	If anyone wants a horse, tell them to try the kitchens. The last one's been dispatched for stewing.
Hugh	[*Approaching him, and speaking in a quiet, insistent voice*] Who would you most want to see in the world?
Richard	Colonel Rigby and his whole besieging army drop into hell.
Hugh	Your brother is here.

Richard *stops sharpening his sword, in disbelief.*

Richard	James?
Hugh	Yes!
Richard	Within these walls?
Hugh	Within a few feet. Waiting for me to call him in.
Richard	[*Putting down his sword*] How is it possible?
Hugh	I believe God has guided his steps to us.
Richard	[*Delighted*] Then God be praised. [*Suddenly suspicious*] But what's he doing here?
James	[*Impatiently*] If you mean to have me hanged, brother, call for assistance. [*Coming into the stable*] But don't leave me to die from the chill, and this stale stink of horse piss.

He takes off his cap. He and **Richard** *look at each other with a mixture of affection and distrust. They cannot resist clapping each other on the back in greeting, but then break away.*

Richard	How in the devil's name are you here?
Hugh	Quick wits! My boys have always had them.
Richard	If you've brought others, I must tell the countess.
James	I am alone, brother. I promise.

Pause, then **Richard** *allows himself to relax.*

Richard	Your word is enough. How are you?

James	Well, thanks to the grace of God. And heartily glad to see you and father alive.
Richard	But how are you inside the castle? There's no breach in the walls.
James	Some of your men surged out an hour ago, hoping to silence our nearest cannon.
Richard	I knew there was to be a sally.
James	While they fought, I stood on the edge...
Hugh	[*Breaking in, excitedly*] He was dressed as a carter, with a cap and staff, so no one would take him for a fighting man.
James	I watched till one of your men fell with a bullet in his guts, then helped his comrades carry him back through the gate. In the confusion, no one thought to question my assistance.
Hugh	[*Proudly*] He had it all planned.
James	I've awaited such an opportunity for days.
Richard	Even so, once inside the gates, surely you were seen?
James	The good Lord must have been protecting me.
Hugh	By chance, I'd come with a cup of spirits for the wounded man. Like a thunderclap, I caught sight of James and almost cried out for joy. Thank God I held my tongue, because at that very moment, one of the countess's cellarmen seemed set on approaching him.
James	I would certainly have been discovered.
Hugh	Before the cellarman reached him, I caught hold of James's arm and brought him here. He's left the encircling army to speak with us.
Richard	Have our prayers finally been answered? Have you returned to your rightful senses?
James	I never left them, brother.
Richard	You are for the king?
James	Yes. I am for the king...

SIEGE

Hugh	[*Breaking in*] God be praised!
James	[*With emphasis*]...under parliament.
	Pause.
Richard	Still a rebel?
James	I only want our country and Church's good.
Hugh	So do we all.
James	Yet you fight for a tyrannical king and the imposition of Romish ways.
Richard	[*Coldly angry*] If that is what you believe of our cause…
James	It is.
Richard	…Then, though it grieves me to say it, your place is not here.
Hugh	Richard, I know in your heart you are happy to see your brother. This is not a time to argue. Since last we met, we have all suffered a dreadful loss. [*To both of them*] Think how your mother would want you to act now.
	Short pause.
Richard	You know she is dead?
James	Word reached me a month ago. I wish the Lord, in His infinite mercy, had let me see her before she was taken.
Hugh	[*To **James***] Till the last, she talked of her sons. In her fever she thought the world was young again and this cursed war had never started. She asked for both of you to be brought in from playing skittles, so she could kiss you farewell.
Richard	[*Accusingly*] I'd ridden twenty miles through blinding rain to bring her comfort.
Hugh	She always spoke of you together. Richard and James. The inseparables.
Richard	I held her hand and soothed her as she left us.
James	So would I, if I'd known in time. This war has not made me a monster… Nor you, I believe.

61

Richard	*[Gently]* You should have been with us, James. Sometimes she looked in my face, only to whisper your name. She saw you in me.
James	Nothing hurts me more than not being there.
Hugh	*[Placing his hands on his sons' shoulders]* We all feel her loss equally.
	*There is a moment of silent closeness between the three of them, before **Richard** slowly pulls away.*
Richard	*[With some bitterness]* It may comfort you to know, in her final sickness, she forgot you'd ever turned your back on her.
James	No!
Richard	On all of us.
James	That was no choice of mine. You know I prayed long and hard for guidance.
Richard	And you were guided to tear our family apart?
James	When King Charles ignored reason and raised his standard at Nottingham, he knew he must tear the whole country apart.
Richard	You call the prating of your raggle-taggle parliament 'reason'?!
James	It is filled with wiser heads than those around the king. If we hadn't stood against him, there'd be no true worship left in the land, only the blasphemies of bishops.
Richard	Isn't it blasphemy to fight against your monarch, whom God has anointed?
Hugh	Keep your voices low!
	He hurries to the doorway and looks out. The argument continues, regardless.
James	Charles is a godless king.
Richard	He is the father of the nation.
Hugh	You will be heard. It's too dangerous to argue. *[Returning, to **James**]* There are rumours your colonel is trying to buy a way into the castle. If you're found you'll be suspected as a courier. We can't answer for your life.
James	Then I'll be brief. I've come with a purpose.

Richard	Which is?
James	Even with her husband in Ireland, the countess has led a brave defence of the fortress.
Richard	She's more than an equal to your commander.
James	I don't question her courage. But we've waited six weeks for a surrender. Every day more of our men fall to your muskets or disease.
Richard	Would the number were doubled or trebled. [*With sincere conviction*] Only sparing you, of course.
Hugh	Amen!
James	You must know your cause here is lost, Richard.
Richard	Your cannons haven't shaken our resolve. Neither will your words.
James	Your Rhinish prince is away in the south and can't break the siege before you starve.
Richard	Starve? Not possible. We have plenty of food left, haven't we, father?
Hugh	[*Hesitantly*] Er… we do pretty well.
Richard	In fact, so that your journey isn't wasted, tell Colonel Rigby we'll trade some fine hams and wine for packs of cards. We need something to pass the time.
James	The whole garrison's well fed?
Richard	Exceptionally so.
James	Yet you and father appear half-starved, and the stables have no horses.
	Richard draws Hugh to one side. They talk in hushed voices.
Richard	Have you spoken of our plight on the way from the gate?
Hugh	No. We discussed nothing. [*Hesitantly*] Nothing of substance.
Richard	[*Suspicious*] Father?
Hugh	He mentioned a proposition.

SIEGE

James   [*Breaking impatiently in*] Brother, if you are determined to stout it out further, without any hope of victory, lives will be needlessly lost on both sides.

            James and Hugh break out of their huddle.

Richard   We do not mean to give in. So it were best you steal away now, while you can.

James   Colonel Rigby will not steal away. His resolve is turning in quite another direction.

Hugh   What do you mean?

James   [*To Richard*] You have always had the countess's trust. You must persuade her, that if she opens the gates now and you lay down your arms...

Richard   What?!

James   ...you may leave unharmed and with honour.

Richard   You would have me counsel surrender?!

Hugh   Richard, hear him.

James   If another day passes, the colonel has said there will be no quarter given at the castle's fall.

Richard   But you have to make it fall first.

James   Hear me out! Not even women and children will be spared if the siege is driven to a bloody end.

Richard   Then you serve with a parcel of murderers.

James   Your own army has done the same before now.

Richard   [*Turning away in disgust*] Hah!

            Hugh catches Richard's arm.

Hugh   [*Softly*] Richard.

James   [*In a more conciliatory tone*] When we were younger, you always had a wiser head than I.

Richard   And still do, to judge from your words.

James	Remember the knife mother gave me when I was ten?
Richard	[*Reluctantly*] Aye.
James	Within a day I cracked the bone handle and flew into a rage, until you calmed me. You said mother mustn't see her gift spoiled. You helped me fashion so good a repair, no crack showed.
Hugh	That's it. Think of the old days. You were such hotheads. You'd wrestle over a misplaced marble or spinning top, as if your lives depended on it. But afterwards you'd be ashamed and make up again, closer than ever.
James	Now help me once more.
Richard	[*Calmly*] I'm pleased you're well, brother. This conflict does not, and cannot, change my deep-held regard for you. But now you must go.
James	You won't speak to the countess?
Richard	Don't ask me to be a traitor!
Hugh	Listen to him, Richard.
Richard	[*Shocked*] What? You take his side?
Hugh	There's sense in what he says.
Richard	For him, yes. If we lay down arms, the castle has been won cheaply. But if we stay the rebels must fight, and I don't believe they have the stomach.
Hugh	It's us who'll have no stomach. How will a morsel of horsemeat feed three hundred?
Richard	Father!
Hugh	Our water is foul. Dysentery has spread through half our men.
Richard	[*Drawing his father again to one side*] Think before you speak. He'll go to Colonel Rigby. 'They're sick, they're dying. Wait a few more days and the castle is ours.'
Hugh	But, Richard…
Richard	[*Angrily, for **James**'s benefit*] If we hold out a little longer, they know Prince Rupert will break the siege. They've only sent James to test our resolve.

Hugh	In two or three days we won't have enough men to defend the gatehouse. We must lose, Richard, and then there'll be butchery.
Richard	Hold your tongue!
James	Don't speak like that to our father!
	Richard grabs hold of James's jerkin.
Richard	I won't have a rebel tell me how to speak!
James	Let go, brother.
	Richard releases him, but the two brothers continue to glare at each other.
	You won't listen?
Richard	Your intentions in coming here were kind, for which I thank you. But your love for me will know, I cannot act the coward.
James	[Short pause] Then the loss of life will be on your shoulders.
	He turns, with regret, away from Richard.
	Father, lead me out.
Hugh	It were better we waited for nightfall.
Richard	[With difficulty] James. I'm afraid you can't leave.
Hugh	It's all right. I know a quiet way.
Richard	[To James] You can't go. Not now that you've learned how ravaged and weak we are.
James	[Short pause] You want to stop me going back?
Richard	If you pass that knowledge to Colonel Rigby, it'll give your troops fresh heart.
James	[In disbelief] What?
Richard	You must stay here.
Hugh	You can't make a prisoner of your brother.
Richard	He can't be allowed to tell the things he's seen.

Hugh	He came out of love for us.
Richard	We have a higher cause than even family to protect.
Hugh	[*Urgently*] James, promise, swear on your mother's memory to hold your peace when you return to the lines.
Richard	Very well. [*To **James***] Your word will be enough for me.

Pause.

James	I can't swear to keep silent.
Richard	Can't?
James	If the colonel knows how desperate your situation is, it might persuade him to grant quarter for a few days more.
Richard	And you would tell him?
James	Yes.
Richard	I won't let you.
James	How will you stop me? Hand me over to be hanged by the countess?
Hugh	No!
Richard	You'll stay as my – our – prisoner. We'll hide you from the garrison and share what little food we have.
James	There's nothing I'd like more. To forget the war and talk of happier times together.
Hugh	We're the only ones lodging here. You'll be quite safe.
James	...but my duty is not to my own wishes. I can't willingly be held prisoner when I have information that may spare many lives.
Richard	You shan't leave.
James	[*Starting to move off*] Adieu to both of you.

Richard *moves quickly to block the way to the door.*

Richard	I'm sorry, brother.

James	Please, Richard. Stand aside.
Richard	No.
	James tries to move round his brother. **Richard** *grabs hold of him.*
James	Leave me be!
	They tussle. **Richard** *succeeds in propelling* **James** *away from the door. They stand, watching each other closely and aggressively.* **James** *raises his staff, threatening to strike* **Richard**.
	Move away, brother, before I'm forced to hurt you.
Richard	If you leave, the castle falls. I can't let that happen.
James	[*Moving forward, with the staff as a weapon*] Move away.
	Richard *backs away slowly and defensively.*
Hugh	Boys, think of your mother looking down from heaven.
	Richard *snatches up his sword and drives* **James** *back.*
	For pity's sake! Think of her!
Richard	Lay down your staff.
James	You'd kill me?
Richard	Lay down your staff!
	James lays down his staff.
Hugh	[*To* **Richard**, *in desperation*] We'll keep him prisoner. We'll take turns in watching him.
Richard	If we do, he'll only wait for a chance to escape.
Hugh	You can't hand him over to be hanged. [*To* **James**] Give your word to stay quietly here with us. You've done all that your colonel can expect.
James	[*Trying to move towards the door*] I will not lie to you, father. My duty is to return, so call for help, or let me go.
	Richard *blocks* **James's** *attempt to leave.*
Richard	You'll force me to use this.

James	[*Trying to move round him*] Do so, if you must.
Hugh	[*To **Richard**]* He's discovered nothing important. He's defenceless. You were never a bully, Richard...
Richard	And I'm not now.
	*He drives **James** back, then picks up another sword and slides it to him. **James** looks at the sword, stunned.*
James	Richard?
Richard	Let God and our own strength decide.
Hugh	[*In despair*] No!
James	[*Picking up the sword*] It's my dearest wish there were another way.
Richard	[*Circling his brother*] And mine.
Hugh	[*Stepping into the middle*] Stop this, boys!
James	Move away, father!
	***James** and **Richard** clash swords, then circle each other.*
Hugh	Hold your swords, I tell you!
Richard	This is not in our hands.
James	It is as God wills it.
Hugh	How dare you say that?
Richard	He has anointed Charles to be our ruler.
James	He wants the country saved from the evil of Rome.
	*He and **Richard** clash swords, then back away.*
Hugh	[*Stepping forward once again*] I saw fighting before either of you whelps. In my first battle, we all cried 'God with us'. The same cry echoed from the rebels' lips. 'God with us'.
James	[*To **Hugh**]* Keep back!
Hugh	Is God fighting himself in this war?

SIEGE

Richard [*To* **Hugh**] Do as James says. We would not hurt you.

Hugh But you'd kill your own brother? Do you believe that God feasts on blood? We're only men! We don't know what He wants.

James He speaks to us clearly, if we're willing to listen.

Hugh Whenever men listen, they hear different things.

Richard and James clash swords.

Stop! I am only a simple man. I don't know what God wants. But I know I want my sons to love each other. I promised your mother I'd see you reconciled.

Richard It's too late.

Hugh Then... [*Stepping between the swords*] ...spare my eyes!

Richard Father...

Hugh Kill me! I'd rather die than see my sons turn on each other like dogs in a ring.

James and Richard try to manoeuvre. Hugh stays between them. There is a complete standoff.

Well? Must blood be shed?

Pause. Almost simultaneously, James and Richard put down their swords.

Richard [*To* **James**] Go quickly. Father will show you an opening where plague bodies were once carried through the walls. It's bramble-grown, but you can still get through.

James nods.

At least you'll keep that secret?

James Yes.

He looks at Richard for a moment, then they hug, before gently breaking away.

Hugh [*To* **James**] Pull your cap down close.

James pulls on his carter's cap.

Richard And remember your staff.

SIEGE

	Richard moves to pick up the staff.
James	[*Trying to reach the staff first*] I have it, brother.
	Richard picks it up.
	Give it to me and I'll go.
Richard	[*Puzzled*] Why's it so heavy?
James	It's thick yew wood.
Hugh	James must hurry.
Richard	[*Inspecting the bottom of the staff*] Stopped up with earth and straw…
James	[*Trying to take it*] Leave it!
Richard	[*Removing the plug from the staff*] …to hide a secret.
	Gold coins spill out.
Hugh	[*Astonished*] Gold? James?
	James moves to pick up a sword. **Richard** knocks it away with the staff and picks up his sword, which he holds to **James's** chest.
	What does this mean?
Richard	[*To* **Hugh**] You said a cellarman was approaching when you first saw him?
Hugh	Well, yes…
Richard	[*Furious*] James was paying the man to betray the gate.
Hugh	No! … James?
James	My first hope was to talk with you. If that failed, the gold was a chance to end the siege without slaughter.
Richard	You lied to us!
Hugh	[*Horrified*] First to turn against the king. But then to deceive your own father…
James	[*Cutting him off*] God will forgive my transgressions. Now, have me hanged or let me go.

71

He moves towards the door. **Richard** *knocks him back with the flat of the sword.*

Richard   Get back, you traitor!

James   Father. Make him let me go.

Hugh turns away. **James** *makes a sudden dash to escape.* **Richard** *lunges at him, stabbing him with the sword.* **James** *falls dead.*

Richard *lays down his sword and kneels beside the body.*

Richard   [Stunned] No! He's dead. I only meant to stop him. [Overcome with grief] Oh, my brother.

Pause.

Hugh   God grant him rest. [Looking up] And me forgiveness, that I ever bred my sons to war.

He kneels down beside **Richard** *and cradles the lifeless body.*

Blackout.

Siege is set in the English Civil War, which took place in the 1640s. The ruling monarch, King Charles I, believed in the 'Divine Right of Kings' – that he ruled through the grace of God, with divine authority over his subjects. The parliament of the time disagreed, criticising the king and refusing to cooperate with his religious and political wishes. Over time this rift resulted in the country taking sides between Parliamentarians ('Roundheads') and Royalists ('Cavaliers'). After a series of bloody battles between 1642 and 1649, the Royalists were crushed and King Charles executed.

Group activities

1. As James heads towards the castle he must be feeling uncertain about what might happen next. Does he have a moment when he thinks he should go back? Devise a short performance in which all the performers stand in their own space and directly address the audience. In the performance, interweave lines that represent:
    *   James's thoughts as he approaches the castle
    *   the accounts of others who witnessed the skirmish outside the gates
    *   Hugh's memories of catching sight of his son dressed as a carter.

    The performers now move to stand in two parallel lines, forming a corridor down which 'James' can walk. As he passes down the corridor towards the castle, other performers offer comments – from James's supporters and his enemies – about the task he is undertaking.

2. To explore the relationship between the two brothers, try the following 'sculpting' activity. First, select two of the group to represent the two brothers. Next, other members of the group take turns to 'sculpt' the two brothers into still images which represent different facets of their relationship. Once a number of ideas have been explored, introduce a third character – that of Hugh, and repeat the exercise for the three of them. Does this make the relationship more complex? Take note of any 'significant' images, and share them with other groups.

3. Read the section of the play in which James tries to persuade his brother to go along with his plan and the two sons talk of their childhood together (from page 64). Stage this section of the play, and, using the convention of flashback, devise short scenes which show key moments in the past lives of the two brothers.

    Start by dramatising the incident of the bone-handled knife mentioned in the text. This incident is used by James to remind his brother of their previous relationship: 'You always had a wiser head than I'. Devise two other scenes from their past when Richard's 'wiser head' might have saved the day.

    Run the whole section of the play interspersed with the three flashback scenes. Does this help us to understand the brothers' relationship – and their predicament?

SIEGE

Performing the play

1. Read the play from James's entrance up to Hugh's line: 'You will be heard.' (page 62). What gives this section its dramatic tension? How might you heighten the tension? In spite of their father's warnings the two brothers continue to argue. What does this tell you about their state of mind at this point in the play?

2. Hugh feels conflicting emotions throughout the play. Read through the play, marking the moments when Hugh's emotional state changes. Choose a section of the play to rehearse and perform, which reveals how Hugh's loyalties are torn between his two sons. What advice will you give to the actor playing Hugh?

3. How should the fight between the two brothers be staged for maximum effect? Realistic fight scenes involving weapons are highly skilled affairs which need training and careful choreography if they are to be executed safely. There are, however, many ways of stylising the fight which might create interesting and powerful dramatic effects. Try out the approaches below.
   - Stage the fight using slow motion with mimed weapons.
   - Break the action of the fight into key moments, and stage the fight as a sequence of still images.
   - Stage the fight with both brothers facing the audience side by side, thrusting and parrying as though they are fighting face to face.

   Construct a sequence using elements of all of the above. Which technique is most effective, and why?

Writing

1. Find out what you can about these key figures of the English Civil War: King Charles I; Oliver Cromwell; Prince Rupert of the Rhine. Write a brief character study of each.

2. Using what you have learnt about the history of the English Civil War, write a diary account of the siege described in the play from two perspectives: a Royalist soldier encamped outside the castle; a female member of the countess's staff.

   Write three entries for each: one in the early days of the siege; one after two or three weeks have passed; one after three months.

   You may find the following websites helpful:

   www.open2.net/civilwar/index.html
   www.bbc.co.uk/history/war/englishcivilwar/index.shtml
   http://en.wikipedia.org/wiki/English_Civil_War

Coming to terms

Characters

Don Wainwright	Head of Science, on the verge of retirement
Timothy Hibbs	An English teacher
Ellen Gilchrist	The deputy head teacher
Janet Ames	A P.E. teacher
Bill Fairclough	The school caretaker
Susan Richards	A student teacher, soon to start her teaching practice

The play is set in the corridor and staffroom of a large comprehensive school, on the last day of the spring term.

SCENE 1

A school corridor. On the wall is a pinboard covered in students' work. In the distance, we can hear a class misbehaving noisily, as **Ellen** *and* **Susan** *enter.* **Susan** *is anxiously clutching her bag.* **Ellen**, *who has been showing her round the school, comes to a halt.*

Ellen So now you've seen the whole school, Susan. I hope our little tour's been helpful.

Susan [Distracted] Er... yes.

Ellen I'm sure you're looking forward to joining us next term. Tinleigh Comprehensive has an excellent record with student teachers.

Susan Oh, good. [Anxiously] That was Nine Beta we just passed, wasn't it?

Ellen Yes.

Susan They seemed terribly noisy.

Ellen [Suppressing her disapproval] Mr Hibbs is a great believer in free expression.

Susan They looked a bit wild.

Ellen	Not at all. In fact, Steve, our last student teacher, had a marvellous time with that class.
Susan	Did he?
Ellen	[*Wistfully*] Such a gifted young man. We're rather hoping he'll join us permanently when he qualifies.
Susan	He must have been good.
Ellen	Excellent. The children adored him. They were so disappointed when he left. [*Tactfully*] Though I'm sure they'll be very pleased to have you.
Susan	I hope so.
Ellen	[*Pointing to the pinboard*] This was Steve's initiative. A poetry wall. He had a real talent for bringing out his pupils' creativity.
Susan	[*Trying to sound enthusiastic*] What a good idea.
Ellen	And he completely revitalised the school magazine.
Susan	While he was on teaching practice?
Ellen	Oh, yes. And stage-managed the school play. And started a cycling club. When he wasn't helping coach the year eight rugby team, that is.
Susan	[*Disheartened*] He was busy.
Ellen	Don't worry, Susan. You don't have to be involved in extra-curricular activities when you're on teaching practice.
Susan	It's all right, Miss Gilchrist. I'd love to... do something
Ellen	Oh, good.
	*There's a particularly loud burst of noise from the offstage classroom, which captures **Ellen**'s attention.*
Susan	That's if I actually come here...
	More noise from the class.
Ellen	[*Not listening to **Susan***] What on earth...
Susan	You see, I did wonder...

COMING TO TERMS

Ellen is keen to move **Susan** away.

Ellen   Perhaps we'd better wait for Mr Hibbs elsewhere. [*Moving offstage*] Let me show you the staffroom.

Susan   Right... Okay.

She hurries off after **Ellen**.

SCENE 2

A cluttered staffroom, with piles of books and folders spilling off tables. There is a door at the back and a notice board on one wall, which is plastered with lists and posters. On one side of the room there are lockers. One of the windows has been recently broken.

Don *is sitting in the most comfortable chair in the room, marking a huge set of worksheets with ruthless efficiency.* **Bill**, *carrying materials to temporarily cover the broken window, comes in.*

Bill   [*Sarcastically*] How do you do it?

Don   [*Without looking up from his marking*] Finally.

Bill   [*Crossing to the broken window*] The last lesson before you retire, and somehow you manage to skive off.

Don   I've been trying to mark, despite the constant breeze through the broken window.

Bill   I'm only clearing the mess. It's the authority's job to replace the glass.

He starts sweeping broken glass into a dustpan.

Don   [*Lightly*] You could be out of a job soon, Bill. A university in America's taught a chimpanzee to use simple tools.

Bill   [*Sweeping up*] Doesn't surprise me. We've had monkeys teaching in this place for years.

Don   [*Lightly*] Chimpanzees aren't monkeys. They're apes. Didn't you learn anything here?

He continues marking, and **Bill** *carries on clearing up broken glass, as* **Janet** *bursts into the room bouncing a netball. She dodges round a couple of chairs and slam-dunks the ball into a waste bin.*

Janet   Goal!

77

COMING TO TERMS

Don   [*Without looking up*] Finished, Janet?

Janet   [*Crossing to the drinks area*] Not quite. I've sent my class into the hall for the head's dismissal, but now there's an under-sixteen's match. If I'm quick, I can snatch a coffee first.

Bill   [*Indicating **Don***] You're not staying for his retirement do?

Janet   It's a home game. I'll keep nipping in and out.

Don   It doesn't matter, if you're busy.

Janet switches on the kettle.

Janet   I'm not missing it for the world, Don. Thirty years' teaching is a real achievement.

Bill lifts a piece of chipboard to see if it will cover the broken window.

Bill   Ten years' actual teaching. Twenty years' skiving in the staffroom.

Don   Thank you, Bill.

Bill continues working through the scene, measuring the hole and marking on the chipboard with a felt-tip pen.

Janet   [*Holding an almost empty coffee jar*] Oh, no!

Don   Some new catastrophe?

Janet   I had almost half a jar left this morning. Now there's only a spoonful left.

Bill   Don't look at me. Caretakers don't have time for coffee breaks.

Don   And I've given up coffee.

Janet   [*Scraping out the last spoonful*] I thinks it's a little bit sad, that's all. If you can't trust the staff, who can you trust?

*She stands waiting for the kettle to boil, as **Ellen** shows **Susan** into the staffroom.*

Ellen   [*To **Susan***] Here we are, the beating heart of Tinleigh Comprehensive. [*Making an announcement*] Everybody, this is Susan Richards, who's joining us on teaching practice next term.

*Janet lollops over and shakes **Susan**'s hand.*

78

COMING TO TERMS

Janet	Welcome to the team, Susan.
Ellen	Janet Ames. P.E. and personal development.
Susan	Nice to meet you.
Janet	I'm sure you'll have a wonderful time here.
Susan	Erm... well, yes, but...
Ellen	She can't wait to start.
Janet	Smashing!
	She returns to the kettle.
Ellen	[*Indicating* **Don**] Don Wainwright. Head of Science.
	Don *raises a hand in greeting then continues marking.*
Susan	Hi.
Ellen	You won't see much of him, I'm afraid. Don's retiring today. A farewell party's starting in the canteen soon.
Don	The dinner ladies' last chance to poison me.
Ellen	[*Indicating* **Bill**] And Bill Fairclough. The whole school revolves round him. He's the caretaker.
Susan	Hello.
Bill	[*Greeting*] All right? [*To* **Ellen**, *indicating the window*] Whoever did this made a right mess, Miss Gilchrist.
Ellen	We think it was an accident with a football. And we've a fair idea of the boy responsible.
Bill	Oh, have you? [*Shaking his head*] I might have guessed.
Ellen	No proof, unfortunately.
Bill	I'll make a few inquiries. And, in the meantime, I'll cut this chipboard to size in my workshop, then get the window boarded up.
Ellen	Thanks.

79

COMING TO TERMS

Bill	No problem.
	He exits, carrying the chipboard.
Ellen	[*To* **Susan**] Mr Hibbs shouldn't be long. [*Moving towards* **Don**] Do you mind if we join you?
Don	Not at all.
	Ellen *and* **Susan** *sit down.* **Janet** *holds up a nearly empty jar of sugar.*
Janet	Miss Gilchrist, is this your sugar?
Ellen	No. I don't take any. [*To* **Susan**] Sweet enough already.
	Susan *forces herself to laugh.*
Janet	[*Helping herself*] I'm sure nobody'll mind me having a little.
Susan	[*Quietly*] I... I've been thinking, Miss Gilchrist...
Ellen	[*Not listening. To* **Don**] No regrets about leaving?
	Don *stops marking and thinks for a moment.*
Don	No.
	He resumes marking.
Ellen	I was just telling Susan what a marvellous impression our last student teacher made here.
Don	[*Not impressed*] Oh, yes. Steve.
Ellen	A real asset to the school.
Janet	[*Heartfelt*] Wasn't he?
Ellen	Such a great help with your netball teams.
Susan	As well as doing rugby, poetry and the school play?
Janet	Yes. The team haven't been the same since he left.
Ellen	No.
	She and **Janet** *sigh simultaneously.* **Don** *glances at them and shakes his head.*

COMING TO TERMS

Susan	[*Quietly, to* **Ellen**] You see, it occurred to me…
Janet	[*Cutting her off*] Still, if we win tonight and the three teams above us all lose by big margins, we won't finish bottom of the league. So it's been quite a good season, really.
	The door bangs open and a dishevelled **Timothy** *staggers in. Unaware of* **Ellen**'s *presence, he clutches the back of a chair and hangs onto it for support.*
Timothy	[*To* **Janet**] What's the point of trying to teach Nine Beta anything? They're thugs.
	Janet *gives a warning cough, which* **Timothy** *ignores.*
Timothy	I've just spent five minutes scraping Kieran Fairclough off the ceiling. He's a complete psycho.
Ellen	[*Standing up. Icily*] Timothy?
Timothy	Hello, Miss Gilchrist.
Ellen	Susan's come in to see you.
Susan	[*Getting up*] Hi.
	Timothy *has no idea who she is.*
Timothy	Hello.
Ellen	…The student teacher you're supervising next term.
Timothy	Oh yes. Terrific.
Susan	You said you'd have some textbooks and a course outline ready for me.
Timothy	[*Having totally forgotten*] Ye-ess… That's right.
Susan	[*Quickly*] It doesn't matter if you haven't, because, as a matter of fact…
Ellen	[*Cutting her off*] Good. I'll leave you to discuss it all.
	She makes to exit, then stops for a private word with **Timothy**.
Ellen	[*Quietly*] Can I suggest not too much doom and gloom about Nine Beta? Steve got on very well with them.

81

COMING TO TERMS

Timothy	[*Through gritted teeth*] Didn't he just?
Janet	[*Coming over*] Miss Gilchrist?
Timothy	[*To* **Susan**] Do you mind if I get a coffee before we start?
Susan	Not at all. You look as though you could do with one.
	She joins **Timothy** *in the drinks-making area. He switches on the kettle, as* **Janet** *catches up with* **Ellen** *near the door. The two conversations can overlap slightly.*
Ellen	What is it, Janet? [*Quietly*] I want to see that everything's ready for Don's party.
Janet	[*Shyly*] I just wondered if you'd heard anything from Steve recently?
Ellen	[*Surprised*] Oh. I thought you'd stayed in touch with him.
Susan	[*To* **Timothy** *anxiously*] So what are Nine Beta really like?
Ellen	[*To* **Janet**] A little bird told me you were going out together.
Timothy	[*To* **Susan**] You'll find out soon enough when you start here.
Janet	[*To* **Ellen**] He did invite me out, only… I haven't heard from him since he left.
Ellen	Oh, dear.
Janet	Still, he's probably had a busy three months, with all the coursework to do. I expect he'll phone when he's got a minute.
Ellen	[*Kindly*] Let's hope so.
	She smiles at **Janet**, *then exits.* **Janet** *takes her coffee and sits near* **Don**.
Susan	[*To* **Timothy**] Are they really difficult?
Timothy	It's best not to worry before you have to.
Susan	The thing is… I'm not absolutely certain I want to come here.
Timothy	No?
Susan	I've been having doubts.
Timothy	[*Searching for some coffee*] Very good things, doubts. Wish I'd had more of them at your age.

COMING TO TERMS

Susan   After talking to Miss Gilchrist… and hearing about your last student…

Timothy   [*Shuddering with distaste*] Steve!

Susan   …I'm not sure I'd make a very good teacher.

Timothy   No? [*Checking in cupboards*] Can you juggle?

Susan   [*Puzzled*] Juggle?

Timothy   Or dance?

Susan   Not very well.

Timothy   Do accounts? Fit tyres? Style hair?

Susan   No.

Timothy   Can you cross Niagara Falls on a bicycle while playing the trumpet?

Susan   I don't think so. Why?

Timothy   If you can do anything other than teach, go and do it. Unless you want to spend the rest of your life hanging on like a prisoner for the end of his sentence, simply to get a pension.

Susan   If you don't like teaching, why not do something else?

Timothy   Now? I'm too old to change.

Susan   No you're not. You're never too old.

Timothy   That, my dear, is inexperience speaking.

               He gives up looking for coffee.

               I don't blame you. It's wonderful to be your age. To have a thousand doors in front of you, each leading somewhere marvellous. The only problem is knowing which one to open first. What you don't notice is time sneaking past on tip-toe while you decide. Then suddenly it's too late. You chose the wrong door and now you can't go back. You've got a family and a mortgage to pay. It would be too selfish, quite impossible, to give your job up. Even though you hate it.

Susan   [*Deeply disheartened*] Oh.

83

Timothy	Of course, I still apply for other things occasionally. Never get anywhere. The smell of failure must taint the form. Employers look at me – fifteen years at the same school, with no serious promotion – and think, there's a man who didn't have his eyes open to the real opportunities when he was young. [Loudly] Janet, have you got any coffee?
Janet	Sorry. There was only a spoonful left.
Timothy	[Sighing] It doesn't matter. [Picking up the empty sugar jar] Someone's pinched the last of my sugar, anyway.
Janet	Oops!

Don *raises his head and tuts with mock-disapproval at* **Janet**.

Susan	[To **Timothy**] But you must have wanted to teach once?
Timothy	Oh, yes. I loved university. Shakespeare, Milton, all the rest. It thrilled me to glimpse eternity through their words. I longed to share that vision. Couldn't wait for my first term here.
Susan	But it didn't work out?
Timothy	Half of the pupils could barely read. The other half didn't care to. And a hat-stand would have had better discipline than I managed. Never mind sharing eternity. Survival's the best I hope for these days.

Timothy *sits down beside* **Janet** *and* **Don**. **Susan**, *feeling forgotten, doesn't know whether to follow him or not. She dithers, trying to pluck up courage to go over.*

Don	[Without looking up] I thought you'd be straight off home, Tim.
Timothy	I'm staying for your do.
Don	Really? That's kind.
Janet	Everyone wants to give you a good send-off, Don.
Timothy	[Half joking] I'm only coming for the drink. I definitely need one.
Janet	[Shyly] There's a chance Steve might turn up.
Don	Oh, good.
Janet	I left a message for him at the college.

COMING TO TERMS

Don	[*Sarcastically*] That's something to look forward to.
Tim	[*To* **Don**] What's the point of marking worksheets now? You're about to escape.
Don	I want to leave things tidy.
	Susan *crosses the room and sits down on the edge of a seat near* **Timothy**.
Susan	You see, I'm not entirely sure about continuing my teaching course.
Timothy	Very wise.
Janet	[*Horrified*] You're thinking of giving up?
Susan	Well… Yes.
Janet	You mustn't! Teaching's a wonderful job.
Timothy	Hah!
Janet	Isn't it, Don?
Don	For some people.
Susan	I've been thinking about it for some time. And then I had a real panic while Miss Gilchrist showed me round.
Timothy	She has that effect on me.
Susan	The school's so big. I felt I was drowning in a sea of faces. The pupils aren't much younger than me. Suppose they won't listen? Suppose I can't control them?
Janet	Everyone worries about that when they start.
Susan	Do they?
Janet	Oh, yes.
	Bill *comes in with the cut piece of chipboard.*
Timothy	About time. I'm getting a crick in my neck from the draught.
Bill	[*Crossing to the window*] I've only got one pair of hands. [*Significantly*] I had to stop and clear up the mess in one of the English classrooms.
Timothy	Ah.

85

Bill	I don't know who's been taking Nine Beta, but they left the place in a right state.
Timothy	[*Innocently*] Did they? Shocking.
	Bill starts taping the piece of chipboard into place, and continues to work through the scene.
Janet	I can remember being so worried on my first day here, Susan. Mum and Dad were really proud of me, getting such a good job.
Timothy	Hah!
Janet	You see, I'd been the first one in the family to go to college. There's a photo of me in my parents' living room. You know, in my cap and gown. Mum said it was the proudest day of her life. And suddenly I had all these kids in front of me in the gym. Staring. Sizing me up. Working out if I could control them. And I thought, what if I can't? What if I let Mum and Dad down?
Susan	But it went all right?
Janet	Yes… Well, not on the first day perhaps.
Bill	We got the door back on its hinges easily enough.
Janet	I admit once or twice I had a little cry in the store cupboard, early on. But I thought that if my parents had faith in me, I should have faith in myself. So I did. I stuck at it. Asked for advice, worked on my lesson plans, and pretty soon, I'd won most of the pupils round. Now I wouldn't swap Tinleigh Comp for anything.
Susan	Really?
Janet	It's so rewarding. Like the under-sixteen's netball. We may have lost more matches than anyone else, but our team spirit's second to none. [*Laughing*] Mum says that, now I've found the perfect job, I just need to find the perfect husband.
	She gives a big, embarrassed laugh. **Ellen** *comes in.*
Ellen	Almost ready in the canteen. Any volunteers to put the wine out?
Timothy	[*Leaping up enthusiastically*] I'm your man, Miss Gilchrist.
Ellen	Thank you, Timothy.

COMING TO TERMS

Timothy   Always happy to help.

He exits.

Janet   I was just telling Susan what a great time she'll have here.

Ellen   Oh, good.

Susan   [*Trying to explain*] You see, Miss Gilchrist…

Ellen   [*Not listening. To* **Janet**] You may find your netball team are a little late getting to the changing rooms.

Janet   I'd better go and round them up.

Ellen   They're all in the car park. They saw Steve arriving.

Janet   [*Hurriedly putting down her coffee cup*] Steve's here?

She dashes to the door.

Ellen   He's just arrived for Don's farewell do, but Janet…

Janet   [*Hurrying out without listening*] See you later!

The door shuts behind her.

Ellen   [*Sadly*] …he's brought his new girlfriend.

Don   [*Looking up briefly*] The beast!

Ellen   I'm starting to have doubts about him, myself. It seems he won't be joining us permanently when he qualifies, after all.

Don   No?

Ellen   He just told me he has an understanding with Hillcroft High. I gather he's planned on going there all along. I'm afraid, under all the charm, he's ruthlessly ambitious.

Don   Should make deputy head in no time, then.

Susan   [*With real effort this time*] Miss Gilchrist?

Ellen   Yes, Susan?

COMING TO TERMS

Susan Supposing a student teacher was having doubts about teaching… when would her practice school need to know?

Ellen Doubts?

Susan Yes.

Ellen Are we talking hypothetically?

Susan Sort of...

Ellen [*Gently*] I should say 'as soon as possible'. But I won't. I can't pretend everyone's suited to the profession, Susan. And if you feel you're not one of them, then perhaps it's better to say so now. But I'd rather you took your time before making a final decision. The college speak quite well of you.

Susan I only got an average grade for my first practice.

Ellen I didn't make a great success of my first one, either.

Susan Honestly?

Ellen Oh yes. [*Wryly*] Of course, it was a long time ago now. I was so determined to keep order in my first lesson, that when I noticed a girl whispering to her friend, I instantly handed out a four-page essay on silence. It was only when the poor thing crumpled into tears that anyone told me her friend had hearing problems, and she was simply trying to pass on what I was saying... It took plenty of mistakes like that before I grew into teaching. [*Kindly*] There's no immediate hurry for your decision.

Susan Right.

Ellen [*Checking her watch*] Don? Bill? Ready for the canteen?

Don [*Indicating worksheets*] I've only a few more to finish.

Bill I'll come down with him. I want to get some tacks in.

Ellen [*Moving to the door*] Don't be too long. You'll be very welcome too, Susan.

Susan Thanks. I'll see.

Ellen goes out. Bill finds tacks and lightly hammers them in place, while Don continues marking. Susan looks round the staffroom with growing horror. Quietly she picks up her bag and starts to creep towards the door.

COMING TO TERMS

Don	[*Without looking up.*] What made you decide to try teaching?
	Susan *stops.*
	There must have been something.
Susan	Well yes, but…
Don	What was it?
Susan	[*Turning back towards* **Don**] It sounds stupid now.
Bill	We won't know if you don't tell us.
Susan	[*Short pause*] Darren. My younger brother.
Don	He talked you into it?
Susan	No. Not exactly.
Don	What, then?
	Susan *decides to confide. She sits down.*
Susan	He's really smart. But he hated school.
Bill	So do lots of people.
Susan	Never really hit it off with his teachers, I suppose. He can come across as cheeky, but he doesn't mean anything by it.
Don	But his teachers thought he did?
Susan	Most of them. Really, he just wanted some help, but he didn't know how to ask in front of his friends.
Bill	I've heard of that happening before now.
Don	So?
Susan	When he fell behind, the other kids called him stupid. That made him lash out. He soon got a name for bullying. One day I found him crying at home. He'd been threatened with exclusion. That's when he asked me to teach him to read.
	Don *puts down his marking and gives her his full attention.*

89

Don	And you did?
Susan	I let him pick out books from the library. Mostly about football. Bored me silly, but it got him started. I didn't mind him taking his time, or making silly jokes when he stumbled over words. I knew, under all the show, he really wanted to succeed. It only took two terms for him to catch up with the rest. He was so pleased when he did. And I was so proud of him. [*Sighing*] But it's a long way from teaching one brother, to controlling a mob of hooligans like Nine Beta.
Don	[*Putting the last worksheet on the pile*] Oh, I don't know. Nine Beta aren't too bad, are they, Bill?
Bill	[*Stopping his hammering*] No. Nothing like the kids here used to be.
Don	That's right. I've taught some real shockers in my time. Absolute terrors.
Susan	Really?
Don	There was one lad in particular – this was years ago – used to torment the life out of the staff. I think I can say every teacher thoroughly hated him.
Susan	Why? What did he do?
Don	Everything. Swore. Stole. Picked fights and bullied. I thought I could handle the tough lads, but he was getting too much even for me. He had a way of picking out your weak spot and working on it.
Susan	Nasty.
Don	Mine was order and organization. I always liked to have my experiments ready when pupils came into class so they didn't grow restless while I set them up.
Bill	He's the same now. Spends hours in his lab preparing.
Don	This lad knew how important that was to me. So it became important to him. One lunchtime I worked right through, setting up a basic receiver and transmitter to show how a radio works. Just before afternoon class, I left the lab for five minutes to register my form. By the time I got back, the whole experiment was smashed in pieces on the floor.
Susan	That's awful.

Don	I knew it had to be him – no one else would have dared – so I made him come back at the end of school. Of course he denied it. Said it was against his human rights to accuse him without proof; he was going to get me arrested; I'd be chucked out of teaching, the lot.
Susan	What did you say?
Don	Nothing. I just let him rant till he got sick of it. He went on for ages.
Bill	It wasn't that long!
Susan	It was you!

Bill *leaves the window, comes over and sits down.*

Bill	Eventually, when I did shut up, he said, 'The capacitor's still all right.' He was pointing at the box where he'd put all the pieces. He told me it needed to be fitted to the coil and showed me how to do it. I'd been expecting him to shout at me. Threw me off, him talking so quiet. Almost polite.
Don	I was too angry to shout.
Bill	I was useless at most things, but somehow I got the capacitor in place real easy. When I looked at the other parts, I thought I could see what to do. But he wouldn't let me stay to finish it.
Don	It was too late and you'd broken too much.
Bill	So I came back the next day. And the day after that.
Don	[*Amused*] Told all your friends you were in lunchtime detention.
Bill	I didn't want them thinking I'd gone soft. Turned out, it wasn't as easy as I thought. I had to keep taking things apart and putting them together again differently. He just let me get on with it. It was so frustrating. I couldn't work out any way to rig the antenna.
Don	Finally, he asked for help.
Bill	That didn't come natural. You didn't, in our house. You handled everything yourself. That was something Dad learned inside, and brought home with him.
Don	Eventually, he got the antenna in place.

COMING TO TERMS

Bill   I couldn't believe it. I switched on, held up the headphones and heard music coming through. For the first time in my life I'd made something work instead of wrecking it.

Don   [*Checking his watch*] We really should be making a move. [*Handing a worksheet to* **Bill**] Do you want to give this to Kieran? He can be looking at it over the holiday.

Bill   [*Reading comments on worksheet*] 'Messy, but definite signs of progress.' I'll give him hell if he's the one who smashed the window. [*To* **Susan**] He's a real pain, my son. But Don's found something in him no one else has. [*To* **Don**] He's going to miss you.

Don   [*Standing up*] Do you know any Latin, Susan?

Susan   No. They didn't teach it at my school.

Don   Not many places do now. I think that's why so few people understand what they're actually saying. Education comes from 'educare'. One of its meanings is to 'bring out'. That's what good teachers do. They don't make pupils learn anything. They simply bring out a hunger for knowledge that's already there. Like you did with your brother.

Susan   I don't know if I can do it with a whole class, though.

Don   Maybe you can't. But it's such a precious gift, perhaps it's worth risking a few weeks at Tinleigh to find out.

Bill   They'll be waiting for you, Don.

     Don *nods. He and* **Bill** *move towards the door.* **Bill** *turns back to* **Susan***.*

     Coming with us?

     Blackout.

92

COMING TO TERMS

Group activities

1. What makes a good teacher? What motivates people to want to teach? In your group, create a list of the qualities that you think make an effective teacher. Compare your list with another group's, and note any similarities or differences.

    Select one of the group to play the role of Susan, who is keen to become a teacher. Have the rest of the group interview her for an English teaching post.

2. Create 'video diaries' for Timothy Hibbs, Don Wainwright, and Janet Ames as they go through a typical day at work. Present them 'live', as if to camera. Focus on the key moments of the day, and their responses to these events.

3. Susan appears to have many anxieties about her forthcoming school placement. In pairs, improvise a scene which takes place between Susan and her best friend, who have gone out for the evening. Susan is honest about her worries. What response does the friend have? Does he or she try to reassure Susan?

4. At one point in the play Timothy Hibbs reveals something of the dilemma he is in, seemingly stuck in a job that he hates. What advice would you give to him? Create a short 'retraining video' for Mr Hibbs, demonstrating what he might do to improve his situation.

5. The five permanent teachers in the play each have different attitudes to their job. Create short monologues for each teacher where they describe their feelings about teaching, and the story of how and why they became teachers in the first place. Perform them as a sequence.

6. Improvise the scene that comes immediately after the end of the play: Don's retirement presentation. Try to capture the poignancy of the moment, the last day of a 30-year career. At the presentation the other teachers are invited to make short speeches in tribute to Don. You may be able to adapt elements of the monologues you devised in activity 5, above.

    What gifts might the other teachers give to Don as retirement presents? Have them give their presents as part of the scene.

    When the speeches and presentations are complete, freeze the action. As the other characters look at Don, what do you imagine they are thinking and feeling? Allow each character a moment to speak his or her thoughts.

COMING TO TERMS

Performing the play

At the end of the play Susan seems to be willing to take up her placement. What do you think reassures her about her decision? Pick three key moments in the play where Susan's attitude begins to change, and rehearse these as short scenes.

Now choose a moment to freeze the action in each of the scenes, to create still images. Holding the freeze, allow each character in turn to speak their private thoughts. Try to isolate the exact moment which most affects Susan.

Writing

Write 'end of term' school reports for the six teachers in the play, including Susan. Comment on their attitude, ability and strengths and weaknesses.

She's behind you

Characters

Katrina	A well-known TV soap actress, playing the Fairy Godmother in the pantomime
Gemma	A trainee journalist
Chris	An actor, playing Mona, one of the Ugly Sisters
Joe	An actor, playing Lisa, the other Ugly Sister
Julie	A young TV soap star, playing Cinderella
Liam	An actor and trained singer, playing Prince Charming

The play is set in the male dressing room of a theatre in the little town of Mablethorpe, during a performance of 'Cinderella'. Both male and female cast members come and go, and stop to pass the time, awaiting their turn on the stage. The room has two doors: one door leads into a corridor which leads onto the stage; the other door is marked 'Wardrobe'.

Gemma is waiting patiently in the dressing room. Through a wall speaker we can hear the pantomime in progress:

Katrina   With no trouble at all, for with these special wishes, Cinders, You shall go to the ball.

Noises: Whoosh, bang! Oohs and ahhs from the audience. Music.

Julie   Oh thank you, Fairy Godmother. Everything is so beautiful.

Julie sings 'This is my moment' (or another appropriate song).

Katrina   [Off, approaching down the corridor] Stupid, filthy animals. Should have them all shot.

Gemma stands up. Katrina bursts into the room dressed as the Fairy Godmother, complete with tiara and magic wand. There is a stain on her costume.

Gemma   Hello, Miss Nicolls. I'm from the Herald.

Katrina   [Suddenly all smiles] How lovely to meet you...

SHE'S BEHIND YOU

Gemma	Gemma.
Katrina	Gemma. Call me Trina, please. I've had a little accident. Never work with children or animals.
Gemma	It's very kind of you all to grant me an interview like this.
Katrina	It's absolutely fine. There's a little knob on the side of that speaker. Turn it down for me, would you?

Gemma *turns the speaker volume right down.*

That's better. Shall we get started, then?

Gemma	It's so strange being in the same room as someone so famous.
Katrina	I'm no different to anyone else, dear, not really.
Gemma	The town is very excited about having you here. How are you finding the place?
Katrina	Before I was offered this engagement, I hadn't heard of Mablethorpe. But now it feels almost like a second home.

Gemma *tries to break in.*

…The people are so warm and so very friendly. And what a beautiful old theatre!

Gemma	You won a Soap Award recently. 'The Nicest Lady in Soapland', wasn't it?
Katrina	Yes. Very kind. Betty Doodle is a gift to play, sometimes complicated, always smiling but underneath there beats the heart of a character with many mixed emotions. The public seem to love her just as much as I do. It's lovely.
Gemma	Do you get a lot of fan mail from the 'Over and Under' viewers?
Katrina	Yes. I try to answer each and every one of them by hand, personally. It's important to remember that real people watch this show. This particular award was very special and meant such a lot to me because it was chosen by the viewers and not some stupid, horrible journalists – no offence, of course.
Gemma	None taken. Journalists can be horrible sometimes. That's sort of why I wanted to go into it, not because I'm horrible of course, it's more to do with wanting to make a difference, do something positive, I suppose…

96

SHE'S BEHIND YOU

Katrina	I don't have a lot of time.
Gemma	Sorry. Your biography in the programme says you appeared in a 'Carry On' film.
Katrina	I was very young. A child actor, actually.
Gemma	What did you play?
Katrina	A crying baby. Joan Simms pushed me down Cricklewood High Street. What a lovely woman.
Gemma	Fantastic. With over thirty years in the business, what would be…
Katrina	Twenty.
Gemma	Sorry. What would be your advice to young people hoping to break into show business?
Katrina	Don't.
	Pause.
Gemma	What do you think of…
Katrina	[*Not listening*] It's such a precarious life, with so much depending entirely on good fortune.
Gemma	What do…
Katrina	…And it's not glamorous either, Jenny. It might look that way from the audience point of view, but there's such a lot they don't see. Look at me now, for instance.
Gemma	I see what you mean.
Katrina	I'm sorry?
Gemma	It does smell a bit. What is that?
Katrina	Manure. I'm afraid I slipped in a little during the transformation scene. Real horses, you see. Have you got enough?
Gemma	There's one other thing, if you don't mind. I really appreciate this, by the way.
	Katrina *gestures to her to continue.*

	The Daily Herald has been running a campaign recently. We've asked our readers to nominate a celebrity to be awarded the Freedom of Mablethorpe. You were nominated.
Katrina	Yes, how lovely.
Gemma	More than nominated – you've received a lot of votes, in fact…
Katrina	[Cutting her off] What can I say? I have already heard about this. The theatre manager slipped a copy of your newspaper my way. I never thought I'd actually win, though.
Gemma	The erm… the voting hasn't quite finished yet. There's another week. I can tell you though, Miss Nicolls, you are doing very well at the moment. Extremely well. The people of Mablethorpe love Betty Doodle.
Katrina	So kind. Who else is in the running?
Gemma	Well, I'm sure you're going to win.
Katrina	Is Julie still up there – Cinders?
Gemma	Yes, and one of the Ugly Sisters – that's because he was born here. Do you have any messages for our readers before the winner is announced?

Katrina speaks clearly into Gemma's Dictaphone.

Katrina	Only to say that I'm having the time of my life and to be awarded the…
Gemma	Freedom…
Katrina	…Freedom of the city… town, would be an enormous honour. May I take this opportunity to wish each and every one of your readers a very happy Christmas and a peaceful, prosperous new year.
Gemma	Thank you very much.
Katrina	My absolute pleasure, Jenny.

Gemma switches off her Dictaphone.

I'd better get this into wardrobe.

Gemma	[Joking] Hello, will you scrape the poo off my tutu, please?

Katrina	[*Unamused*] They have a spare.
Gemma	[*Abashed*] I'm sorry, I didn't mean to be...
	Katrina *exits through the door marked 'Wardrobe'.* **Gemma** *takes a deep breath. The other door bursts open, conveying the sound of enthusiastic applause from the stage. Enter* **Joe** *and* **Chris**, *dressed as Mona and Lisa, the Ugly Sisters. They are both wearing extravagant ball gowns.*
Joe	That Act-One overture went on for a fortnight. What's up with the M.D.?
Chris	He's been in the pub since dinnertime. Seventy-eight today, can you believe that?
Joe	He doesn't look a day over ninety.
Chris	'Bosom Buddies' felt like a funeral march. Talk about drag!
Joe	I 'ope you're not eludin' to me, dreary.
Gemma	Hello.
	Joe *starts.*
	I'm sorry.
Chris	Who's this?
Joe	Are you new?
Gemma	I'm from the Herald. Gemma...?
Chris	Oh, hello. Make yourself at home.
Gemma	Thank you. Great outfits, by the way.
Joe	These old things?
Chris	You should see us in our costumes.
Joe	Please be gentle with us, Gemma. My sister and I get awful snippery round members of the press. Just so you know, we only do 'hinterviews' with the most quality of newspapers, so don't be fishing for filth...
Chris	We don't do kissin' and tellin', either.

SHE'S BEHIND YOU

Joe   Only cos we've never been kissed. Well, she hasn't. And please, don't insult us by askin' for scandalous, squalid stories. We never reveal anything about the nasty, vile habits of our co-stars.

Chris   Not unless you pay us, of course.

Joe   We're not ones for tittle-tattle, and we don't like gossip.

Chris   So who do you want to know about?

Gemma   I'm not sure, really.

Joe   You must have a favourite – someone who stands out a bit, someone with that little extra sparkle?

Gemma   I suppose…

Joe   It's me, isn't it?

Chris   You?

Joe   Is it?

Gemma   What about Cinderella? She seems very nice.

Chris   Cinderella.

Joe   Cinderella. Such a pretty girl. Lovely teeth.

Chris   Lovely hair.

Joe   Such a shame they're not her own. And what exquisite tattoos.

Gemma   [*In disbelief*] No!

Chris   Neck to ankles, I'm afraid. That girl is seriously inked.

Joe   They struggled to find tights thick enough. And how strong she is!

Chris   Such powerful little jaws.

Joe   She bites. I'm scratched to ribbons under this frock, and all for daring to suggest she lay off the cigars a little.

Julie appears in the doorway, as Cinderella. She is wearing a beautiful ball gown. **Chris** *and* **Joe** *pretend not to notice her.*

SHE'S BEHIND YOU

Gemma   You're pulling my leg...

Joe   Certainly not.

Gemma   I bet you like her, really.

Joe   Like her? Do we like Cinderella? She's alright if you get her on a good day, so long as you stay up wind.

Chris   She smells.

Joe   Chips and cider.

Chris   But apart from all that, she's absolutely...

Julie   Adorable?

Chris and *Joe* feign terror and try to hide from *Julie*, who shakes *Gemma's* hand.

You must be Gemma. I see you've already met my lovely sisters.

Gemma   You heard all of that?

Julie   And worse. They're on their best behaviour tonight. It's because you're here.

Gemma   It's a great show. I brought my whole family on your opening night. They loved it. You've got a fantastic voice.

Joe   Thank you.

Julie   She was talking to me, thank you.

Joe   Such vanity.

Gemma   Have you done anything on the West End?

Julie   I queued for a bus once.

Gemma   Had you been for an audition or something?

Julie   No, I just thought I'd get that one in before either of these two. You're from the Herald, aren't you?

Gemma   Yes. Did you get my letter?

Julie   I did. It was lovely, too. Most journalists just expect you to drop everything.

101

SHE'S BEHIND YOU

Joe   We try to oblige.

Chris   Speak for yourself.

Julie   Leave it out, ladies.

Gemma   I'm not really a journalist. I am from the Herald, but they haven't given me a job yet – well, not as a reporter or anything. My step-mum does an agony aunt page. She got me in. I hope you don't mind.

Julie   Why should we mind?

Gemma   I'm a cleaner, really, and I make coffee sometimes. The editor said he'd give me a chance if I took him something newsworthy. I thought interviews with the cast of Cinderella might do it, especially as three of you are runners-up in the Freedom of the Town campaign. That was my idea, actually.

Joe   You'd think that would be enough for you to get a foot in.

Gemma   The editor doesn't know. I ran the idea by my step-mum first and, well…

Chris   She pinched it?

Gemma   Not exactly. She didn't think he'd take it seriously.

Chris   She pinched it.

Julie   If there's anything we can do to help, just say the word, okay?

Gemma   Thanks. That's really nice.

Joe   I think we should tell her about Hot Pants. She'd be offered her own column.

Chris   No. The girl wants to be a journalist, not a gossip-monger.

Liam enters, dressed as Prince Charming, in a white and gold military-style jacket, with striped trousers tucked into riding boots. He sits down and sighs deeply.

Julie   Are you going to say hello?

Liam   Hi.

Liam fixes his make-up in a mirror. Pause.

Gemma   I'm Gemma. [Short pause] From the Herald.

102

SHE'S BEHIND YOU

Liam *looks at* **Gemma** *intensely. He manages a smile.*

Liam	Nice to meet you, Gemma.

Pause.

Gemma Are you enjoying the show?

Liam Not really.

Joe A little ray of sunshine, isn't he.

Liam You're here for Julie and Katrina, I suppose?

Gemma We hardly ever get celebrities in Mablethorpe, especially two at once. It's a bit of a happening, really.

Liam There's that word again.

Gemma Mablethorpe?

Julie Liam's got a thing about celebrity.

Joe One in particular.

Chris *gives* **Joe** *a nudge.*

Gemma It must be nice to work with such well-known people. There's Trina Nicolls from 'Over and Under'. And Julie's been in 'Family Circles' since it started. They're household names.

Joe So's Andrex.

Julie Watch it, you.

Gemma How old were you when you got the part?

Julie Eleven.

Liam I'd loved to have been a part of this profession when it was still worth something.

Chris Here we go.

Liam All I ask is for once to be judged on my ability rather than how much TV I've done.

103

SHE'S BEHIND YOU

Gemma   Do you mind if I record this?

Liam   Go ahead.

Gemma   What TV have you done?

Liam gives Gemma a hard stare.

Joe   Not the best start.

Gemma   Sorry.

Julie   Liam trained at the Royal College of Music.

Gemma   You are a fantastic singer. You're brilliant.

Liam   Thank you.

Gemma   My gran loved you.

Chris and Joe wince and exchange looks.

Liam   Great. She'll be cock-a-hoop when you tell her I was in a commercial.

Gemma   Which one?

Chris and Joe launch into their interpretation of the TV advert.

Chris   [As a fussy housewife] Oh Rover, what a naughty dog you are, jumping all over Mummy's new furniture.

Joe   [As her husband] That's alright, darling, it's been treated with Stainaway, the brand new pet-resistant coating.

Chris   Is it husband-resistant, too?

Gemma   That was you? You were the husband?

Liam   I was the dog.

Gemma   My gran loves dogs.

Joe   Not good.

Gemma   My dad liked you, though. He said you were wasted.

Chris   Better.

104

Gemma	He said with a voice like that, you should be doing musicals or something. He thought you were an opera singer.
Joe	She's good.
Liam	My first role was Alfredo in 'La Traviata'.
Gemma	Fantastic.
Liam	Do you know it?
Gemma	Well, I've... No, sorry.
Liam	It went to Japan. Since that finished, I've done a voice-over, the Stainaway ad, and then perhaps my most humiliating job to date...
Julie	You don't mean this?
Liam	I was a singing banana in a supermarket. This comes a close second.
Chris	Thanks a bunch.
Liam	In the space of twelve months, I've gone from a twenty-piece orchestra to drums and an organ. This time last year I'd have been warming up for my aria at the top of Act Two. I'm now about to wow the east coast of England with 'Do You Think I'm Sexy?'.
Gemma	My gran thought you were.
Liam	How flattering.
Gemma	My sister wants to marry you.
Liam	Does she?
Joe	[*Teasing*] Was that a smile?
Chris	Where?
Gemma	I suppose you're already married?
Liam	No. I have my eye on someone, though. Did have... Maybe I should meet your sister.
Gemma	You'd have to wait a while.

Liam	We're here for another month.
Gemma	She's six.
Julie	You'll have to stick with the one you've got.
Joe	Who is the lucky lady then, Liam?
Liam	No comment.
Julie	Come on. Is it someone we know?
Joe	Someone in the cast, perhaps?
Chris	Stop it.
Liam	I'd rather not say.
Joe	It'd be a lovely scoop for Gemma. Passion at the Grand.
Liam	There's no story. She's not interested.
Chris	You've asked her?
Liam	Can we change the subject, please?
Joe	He's bleak enough when he's happy, the thought of putting up with him in this state for the next four weeks is giving me the shivers. [To *Julie*] Can't you reconsider?
Julie	Me? Are you having me on?
Joe	Whoops. There I go again, putting my size elevens in.
Chris	Accidentally on purpose.
Liam	I wasn't going to say anything. I'm fully aware of how disgusted you must feel.
Julie	Why should I feel disgusted?
Liam	Lets say, a little birdie told me.
Julie	Told you what?
Liam	That you think I'm abhorrent. That you'd rather have your eyes gouged out than even consider a relationship with me.

SHE'S BEHIND YOU

Chris	Sounds like a fairy story to me.
Joe	You could be right.
Liam	What else? Ah yes, even the thought of me kissing you on the walk-down every night makes you feel physically sick.
Joe	There's worse places to be kissed.
Julie	I haven't said any of this.
Gemma	What's a walk-down?
Chris	It's at the end, when everyone comes down for a bow.
Gemma	Right.
Julie	Liam, I promise I haven't said any of that stuff.
Liam	You're not going to admit to it with a reporter in the room.
Gemma	I'm not really a reporter.
Julie	It isn't true.
Liam	You don't hate me, then?
Julie	Of course not. I wondered why you've been acting so strange.
Liam	You like me, then?
Julie	Yes. You're okay. You're a nice enough bloke.
Liam	Nice enough?
Julie	Very nice. You're talented…
Joe	Cheerful…
Liam	So what's the problem?
Julie	There isn't a problem.
	Chris and Joe are transfixed. Gemma is trying not to listen.
Liam	Do you think there's a chance we might… What I mean is, would you consider… Do you think we could…

Joe	Say yes, whatever it is. Please!
Julie	You're a great bloke, Liam.
Liam	You're a great girl... woman. I've adored you since the first time you walked into the rehearsal room. I think you're amazing. Beautiful.
Gemma	My granny would be over the moon if she was in your shoes. Or slippers, even. Sorry.
Liam	I'm so relieved. I really thought you hated me.
Julie	I don't hate you, at all. *[Short pause]* You're not the type of person I'd have a relationship with. Not really.
Liam	You could give me a chance, at least. Come for a drink somewhere, a meal maybe?
Julie	I don't know what to say.
Joe	'Yes' might be good.
Julie	Sorry, Liam.
Liam	*[Sarcastically]* That's not at all humiliating. I should have realized. Someone like you wouldn't be interested in someone like me.
Julie	What's that supposed to mean?
Liam	Someone who isn't a name.
Julie	That's ridiculous.
Liam	I shouldn't have said anything.
Gemma	You don't have to worry about me. I won't repeat any of it.
Liam	Of course you will. You're a reporter.
Julie	There's no need to take it out on her.
Gemma	It's fine. Really. Here.

Gemma *rewinds her Dictaphone, to the sound of garbled squeaky voices. She hits the 'play' button, and the Dictaphone plays:*

Julie	Liam trained at the Royal College of Music.
Gemma	You are a fantastic singer. You're brilliant...

Gemma rewinds a little further, then stops the machine.

Gemma	All gone.
Joe	Bang goes your big break, lovey.
Gemma	I want to be a news reporter. I'm not into embarrassing people. Not unless they really deserve it.
Chris	Good girl.
Julie	I've got a story for you. This one should get your editor's attention.
Gemma	Is it about the theatre closing?
Julie	I didn't know it was.
Gemma	Yes. They're knocking it down after your show ends.
Julie	No!
Gemma	I was going to suggest a 'save the theatre campaign'. My step-mum thought it was a bad idea.
Joe	There's a surprise.
Gemma	She didn't think anyone would be bothered.
Chris	Look at all the people here tonight.
Julie	The people here every night.
Gemma	They weren't even going to have a pantomime this year; that's what my dad said. Then they realized they could use the profits to have the place demolished.
Julie	That's horrible.
Gemma	The land is worth more without the theatre standing on it. That's what the council says.
Chris	Cash versus culture.

109

Liam	I'd hardly call this culture.
Chris	What would you call it? This place would have gone under a long time ago if it wasn't for shows like this. 'La Traviata' doesn't do it for everyone. I saw my first-ever pantomime at this theatre. It's hardly the most elevated form of entertainment, I admit, but it's certainly the most popular. You were keen enough to take the job, I remember.
Gemma	I saw my first show here, too. 'The Wizard of Oz'. I was about seven. My mum made me a Dorothy outfit. Whenever it was windy, I'd beg her to let me go and play on the dunes. I wanted to get caught in a hurricane so I could meet the Lion. I loved the Cowardly Lion.
Chris	Put 'em up!
Joe	There's no place like Mablethorpe, Dorothy.
Gemma	That wasn't you?
Chris	That was me. And this was the Tin Man.
Joe	Slightly tarnished these days.
Gemma	Amazing. I can't believe it was you. Do you always work together?
Joe	Pretty much.
Chris	More since we started producing.
Joe	I think, between us, we've played in every theatre there is. In the U.K. at least. There seem to be fewer of them as each year goes by.
Chris	And we're slogging our guts out so they can send this one the same way.
Julie	It's sick.
Liam	We're going to be the last people to perform here.
Chris	We're making history.
Joe	We are history.
Liam	Now who's being cheerful?
Chris	This place reminds me of the Neptune.

Joe	Hanover Street, Liverpool. That was a fleapit. Remember those doors?
Chris	Solid iron. There were three on each side of the stage, bright red. They'd take your arm off if you weren't careful.
Joe	And when they closed they'd send a force-ten gale through the place. Ebenezer was late for the cave scene one night, he came careering into the wings, the force from the doors made the backdrop billow like a hurricane had hit – it sent Aladdin's lamp shooting into the orchestra pit. The harpist ended up flat on her back.
Chris	Nothing new there. Lily liked a bit of a tipple.
Liam	You had a harpist?
Joe	Aladdin had to climb down and prise the lamp out of her harp. The audience were in pleats. They couldn't see what was going on, of course. Just the sound of Lily shouting, 'Get your grubby hands off my instrument'.
Gemma	[Laughing] That wouldn't have sounded too good.
Chris	It sounded terrible – somewhere between an angry cat and the Tardis taking off. Ruined the tension.
Joe	Ruined the harp. We had to pay for another.
Gemma	I didn't know you were both producers.
Julie	They're producing this.
Chris	Kind of.
Gemma	You must have known about this place, then?
Chris	They've certainly been shady about booking the place for next year.
Joe	Now we know why.
Julie	How does it all work?
Joe	The council gives us so much to put a show on for them, usually a relative pittance, then they take the lion's share of the box office.
Chris	We provide the script, cast it, get a crew together, musicians, set, costumes, publicity. Most of the budget goes on the names.

Julie	I feel guilty now.
Chris	That's just how it works, there's no need to feel bad. You're getting the tickets sold.
Julie	And Trina.
Joe	They're not coming to see us, that's a fact.
Liam	Typical.
Chris	Places like this were the heart of the community at one time. They brought people together. It's like they have a soul, especially the old ones.
Liam	It's so depressing. Soon there'll be nowhere to play at all.
Joe	And then, Prince Charming, your humiliation will be over.
Julie	That wasn't the story I had in mind. It's not as important but you might get it past your editor. I'm not supposed to know this yet, so there won't have been any press releases.
Gemma	It sounds big.
Julie	I'm leaving the show.
Chris	Not this one, I hope?
Julie	'Family Circles'.
Chris	You're joking?
Julie	They're writing me out, it's just been decided.
Chris	Are you sure?
Julie	Trina knows one of our writers.
Gemma	Do you know how it's going to happen?
Julie	My character works on her boyfriend's dad's farm.
Liam	Dwain.
Julie	I didn't know you watched it?
Liam	Only when it's on.

SHE'S BEHIND YOU

Julie	Sarah's on the farm – that's me, well, my character. Anyway, I'm mucking out in the cowshed when a low-flying fighter jet scares all the cows and I get trampled to death.
Joe	Talk about rubbing your face in it.
Gemma	Are they getting rid of Dwain as well?
Julie	No. They're bringing a supermodel in. She finds me in the cowshed as I'm about to draw my last breath and tells me all about the affair her and Dwain have been having. I try to speak but I can't cos I've got a load of muck in my mouth, then she tells me she's told Dwain I've been fooling around with old Mister Tingle.
Liam	That's an absolute lie. Sarah would never do that – she loves Dwain. He loves her.
Julie	It's only what the writer said.
Chris	And this all came from Katrina?
Julie	It was good of her to tell me, really. At least I can start looking for other stuff.
Gemma	I'm sure you'll be fine. You're a fantastic actress.
Julie	I'm not so sure.
Joe	It didn't do Kylie any harm.
Gemma	You could go into music?
Julie	Obscurity, more like. Make the most of it while I'm still newsworthy.
Gemma	I can't believe you'd let me have a story like this.
Julie	You deserve a break. It won't do me any harm, will it?
Chris	[*With emphasis*] Maybe Gemma would like a quick tour backstage. It might be the last chance she gets.
Gemma	That would be great.
Joe	They should have finished setting for Act Two now. I'll get the S.M. to show you around. Come on.

113

SHE'S BEHIND YOU

Gemma	Thanks again, Julie.
	Julie smiles back at Gemma. Joe escorts Gemma out of the dressing room.
Joe	Watch your step. The horses haven't been house-trained.
Gemma	So I've heard.
	Joe and Gemma exit towards the stage. Chris takes his wig off.
Julie	What are you going to do next year, Chris?
Chris	No idea.
Liam	You're not going to throw in the towel, are you?
Chris	Something'll turn up, it usually does. I need to make a call. Can I leave you two in the same room?
Liam	I'll be the perfect gentleman.
Chris	It's her I'm worried about.
	Chris exits towards the stage.
Liam	Am I miserable?
Julie	Yes.
Liam	When did she tell you all this?
Julie	A few days ago. I was going to keep it quiet, then I thought, what's the point? If I'm finished, I might as well let everyone know about it.
Liam	You're not finished. You're fantastic.
Julie	Who told you all that stuff about me, Liam?
Liam	I don't want to cause any trouble.
Julie	I don't know which is worse, that someone has been making all sorts of stuff up about me, or that you were willing to believe them.
Liam	She made it sound so convincing.
Julie	She?

114

Liam	I had to talk to someone. I mentioned it to Joe; he said that I should just ask you outright. I couldn't. It's like being back at school again. I've tried. Every time I opened my mouth, something stupid would come out of it.
Julie	Joe wouldn't have said that I hated you.
Liam	It was Trina.
Julie	Trina?
Liam	I didn't say anything to her. She said she could see it in the way I looked at you. It took me by surprise, to be honest. Trina and I had words on the opening night. She hadn't really spoken to me since then. I was glad to be back in her good books. That's all forgotten now. I told her how I felt about you, she listened and smiled, then she put her hand on my knee, apologized, and told me you'd been saying all those things about me.
Julie	Why would she do a thing like that?
Liam	She's nasty. I know that now.

*Behind **Liam** and **Julie** the door marked 'Wardrobe' is gently pushed open a crack. **Katrina** stands listening at the door. There is a wet patch on her tutu.*

	I didn't see it at first. I thought she was one of the nicest people I'd ever met. She always made the effort to talk to me in rehearsal. She paid me loads of compliments. I was telling her about how awful my digs were – this was only on the second day. She even offered to pay for a room in her hotel.
Julie	I think I know where this is heading. What did you have words about?
Liam	She asked me to meet her in her dressing room after the first show. I knocked on the door, went in. She lunged at me.
Julie	That's gross.
Liam	I managed to get away. After a bit of a struggle. I mentioned it the next day and she tried to suggest that I'd started it. She's been horrible about Chris and Joe, as well. She said they can afford to pay me three times as much as I'm on. And she said they'd sacked those dancers for no good reason and forced them to give their wages back.

SHE'S BEHIND YOU

Julie	Trina had those dancers dismissed; she'd accused one of stealing and the other… I think you can guess. Chris told me not to repeat that, by the way.
Liam	She's just nasty. If it wasn't for Chris and Joe, she wouldn't be here. They're paying her ten thousand pounds a week, and she's saying things like that about them.
Julie	Ten grand a week, is that what she said?
Chris	[Off, *talking on his mobile phone*] Okay, thanks Carol. Just thought I'd run it by you. Cheers, now.

Chris enters. Katrina silently closes the 'Wardrobe' door.

Julie	Do you think Trina's really earning all that?
Liam	She said you were on three.
Chris	I suppose this is Trina again? She has no way of knowing how much anyone is earning. And, just for the record, you cost a lot more than she does.

Chris sits down. Katrina appears again behind the door.

Julie	Sorry.
Chris	You're a bigger name. Much bigger. You're not being written out of your show, by the way. I've just called your agent. As I thought, you're in the middle of a five-year contract, and they've already made an offer for the next five.
Julie	You mean she made it all up? What about Gemma? I gave her the story.
Chris	I'll have a word.
Liam	Poor kid, there's another one she can't use.
Julie	Fancy making up a horrible thing like that.
Chris	You've fallen foul of old Hot Pants again.
Julie	Everyone thinks she's so nice.
Chris	Nicest lady in Soapland.
Liam	You deserve to be a bigger star than she is. You've got a great voice, you never step over anyone's lines, and you're always word perfect.

Chris	Madam makes hers up as she goes along.
	***Katrina** is furious. She attempts to sneak to the other door to make her exit.*
	'Glass kippers'. I could've killed her for that one, on press night as well. No wonder she got such stinking reviews.
Liam	Why do you call her Hot Pants?
Chris	Liar, liar…
All	Pants on fire!
	*They laugh. **Katrina** tries to make a dash for the door as **Joe** enters. They collide. **Julie**, **Liam** and **Chris** turn round.*
Chris	How long have you been there?
Katrina	Long enough. Get out of my way.
Julie	I'd like a word with you. What do you think you're playing at?
Katrina	I was only having a little joke. How was I to know you were going to take it seriously? It isn't my fault you don't have a sense of humour.
Julie	And what about all the stuff you said to Liam?
Katrina	I haven't said anything to Liam.
Liam	She's jealous.
Katrina	Jealous? Of a jumped-up little trollop like her?
Liam	She can run circles round you.
Katrina	I seriously doubt that. I have been in this business twenty years.
Joe	And the rest.
Julie	Why do you have to be so nasty to everyone? What have we ever done to you?
Joe	She's an addict.
Katrina	I am no such thing.

Joe	Some poor sods take to the bottle, others go for various chemicals. Hers is conflict. She can't get enough of it. That's what comes of having everything your own way for years.
Katrina	Rubbish.
Joe	And realizing that it's not going to last forever. There's nothing more distasteful than a star that refuses to fade. I've often thought it must be better never to have had it at all, than to turn into something like this.
Katrina	At least I made it. I got somewhere, that's more than can be said for either of you two. Look at yourselves. You're grotesque, you're hideous.
Joe	This washes off. You're stuck with yours. You're on your way out and you can't face it.
Katrina	I'll be around for a long time yet.
Chris	Trina's the one that's been axed. That's why we got her cheap. That and her terrible reputation, of course.
Katrina	They love me out there. I'm the nicest lady in Soapland.
Julie	They love Betty Doodle. In exactly the same way they love 'Sarah'. We don't enter into it, we don't really exist. It's a game. The trouble is, you've been playing it so long, you think it's all real. You actually believe it.
Joe	You're about as nice as carbolic.
Katrina	Turn on me, why don't you? You're vile, all of you. I've never been so insulted. Come on, keep going. Or have you finally run out of lies? It's true what they say. Never work with children or desperate amateurs. I should sue, it'll serve you right. You're in breach of contract. You're not supposed to say anything about me leaving 'Over and Under', which was entirely my choice by the way.
Chris	She's been axed.
Katrina	I'll take you for every penny you've got. You need me. This show needs me. Do you want me to walk. Do you? I will. I'll walk now, even.
Chris	That would be inconvenient.

Katrina	Apologize. Everyone. [*To* **Chris**] You can start.
Chris	Fairies first. You can apologize to the two male dancers, the A.S.M., those three stagehands, the lad who sold the programmes...
Liam	Me.
Joe	Not him as well?
Chris	You're old enough to be his grandmother.
Katrina	They're all liars. I've had enough. I've hated every second of it. I hate this town, I hate this building. I hate you, all of you. Call yourself producers? The only funny thing in this theatre is the audience. It's embarrassing. Whatever possesses them? Turning up in their droves, sitting there night after night, in their cheap clothes, scoffing sweets, dropping ice cream everywhere. If you didn't have me, those tatty little seats would be empty. [*Indicating* **Julie**] She's just a kid. No one wants to see her, she's only been famous for five minutes. This whole place gives me the creeps. There must be something wrong with them to want to live in a dump like this. It's bad enough having to visit.
Chris	I was born in this town.
Katrina	That explains a lot.
Joe	Those people are paying your wages.
Katrina	The sooner they pull this place down the better. That's the best news I've heard all day. If I hadn't already arranged for an extremely fast car to get me out of here the very second the final show comes down, I would gladly start the demolition myself.
Chris	I thought you were leaving tonight.
Katrina	I've reconsidered. My professionalism won't allow it.
Joe	Don't let that stop you. We could have you replaced by tomorrow.
Katrina	You'd never get away with it. Imagine the headlines. 'Ugly Sisters sack the nicest Lady in Soapland'. I am this close to being awarded the Freedom of Mablethorpe. There'd be an uproar.
Liam	What time is it?
Julie	I'm not sure.

Liam	Shouldn't we have had beginners by now?
Julie	Nothing's come through on the monitor.
Katrina	Some idiot's turned it down.

Katrina turns the volume back up on the speaker. The sound of an irritated stage manager comes booming out on the speaker over the Act Two overture.

S.M.	[Voice over] Stand by flies. Stand by lecs. Act Two beginners on stage now, please! All of you!

The actors fly into action and hurl themselves out of the dressing room. There's a tap on the door.

Gemma enters the empty dressing room. She looks around and finds her Dictaphone, and is surprised to find that it is recording. She rewinds, turns the wall speaker down low again, and listens to the words that have been caught on the tape. On the Dictaphone:

Chris	Trina's the one that's been axed....

Gemma winds forward. On the Dictaphone:

Joe	You can apologize to the two male dancers, the A.S.M., those three stagehands, the lad who sold the programmes...

Gemma winds forward again:

Katrina	I hate this town, I hate this building...

Gemma winds forward again:

This whole place gives me the creeps. There must be something wrong with them to want to live in a dump like this. It's bad enough having to visit.

Gemma winds forward again:

I am this close to being awarded the Freedom of Mablethorpe.

Gemma stops the Dictaphone.

Gemma	I don't think so.

Gemma takes out her mobile phone and makes a call.

[Into mobile] Hello, Mr Drayton, it's Gemma. I think I've got a story.

Blackout.

SHE'S BEHIND YOU

Class discussion

The origins of pantomime can be traced back to the Italian *Commedia dell'arte* of the 16th century. Thanks to its most famous character, the foppish clown Harlequin, the Italian tradition became very popular in England, and would eventually evolve into modern-day pantomime.

Have you ever been to a pantomime? Pantomimes have particular dramatic conventions that are repeated in each production. Make a list of as many of the traditional elements and characters as you can think of.

Group activities

1. Pantomimes are usually based on a fairy tale or children's story. In your group, choose a pantomime with a story you all know. Now choose a scene to devise that will allow you to explore some of the pantomime conventions you have listed. You might want to include a song-and-dance routine, humour and jokes, slapstick comedy, exaggerated characters, men dressed as women (the dames), women dressed as men (the principal boy). Think about the exaggerated acting style and gestures common to lots of pantomimes. Include a section that allows those watching to join in – known as audience participation.

2. Joe and Chris are actors playing the Ugly Sisters in the pantomime. Pantomime dames can be played by either men or women, and very often a performance will include a number of slapstick comedy routines as well as lots of verbal wordplay. The term slapstick comes from a wooden bat made up of a pair of wooden slats carried, originally, by a mischievous character such as Harlequin. When someone is hit by a slapstick it produces a loud noise – but without hurting the actor.

   In pairs devise a short comic sequence that the Ugly Sisters might perform in a production of Cinderella. Your comic routine might be physical, such as applying great mounds of make-up, fighting over the last sweet in a jar or learning a complicated dance routine. They may be based on clever wordplay – arguing, for instance, over who is the most beautiful or has the most admirers.

3. Although the play is largely comic, and features fast-paced, humorous dialogue, there are also moments of contrasting sadness and dramatic tension. Make a list of the serious themes and storylines that run through the play – for example: Liam's love for Julie and her rejection of him.

121

In your group, go through the script and find moments where the more serious aspects of the dramatic action are interrupted by comedy or witty dialogue. Why do you think the author combines serious and comic elements in this way?

Performing the play

1. Read the opening of the play, up to Joe and Chris's entrance (page 99). What do we learn about Katrina's character? In pairs, rehearse and perform Gemma's interview with Katrina. At different times Katrina lets her façade slip and exposes a more bitter side to her character. How would you make this clear to an audience, without making it too obvious and heavy-handed?

   Gemma is in awe of Katrina, but are there moments when she is surprised by the sharpness of Katrina's replies? The characters often interrupt or cut off each other's lines. What effect does this have on the pace of the scene, and what does it tell us about the status of the characters?

2. Chris and Joe's comic banter is delivered in a sharp and pithy manner. They seem to have an answer for everything and add humour to the exchanges between other characters. What demands does this kind of dialogue make on the actors playing these roles?

   Read some of the quick-fire dialogue. In small groups, experiment with delivering the lines with varying pace and emphasis until you find a comfortable and effective performance style. Is this similar to the acting style you experimented with during the pantomime activities, or is a more naturalistic or subtle characterisation and delivery of the lines more effective?

Writing

At the end of the play, the cast have rushed back onto the stage. Gemma is left alone contemplating what she has just witnessed in the changing room. She has recorded evidence that Katrina is not the loveable person that the public thinks she is.

On a piece of paper, design the front page of the Mablethorpe Herald. Writing as Gemma, compose a headline that will lead your article. Now write the front-page story describing and commenting upon everything Gemma has just learned in the theatre. Remember that Gemma does not want to embarrass people 'unless they really deserve it.' What does she do in Katrina's case?

Delinquent

Characters

Dom	a boy, aged 15, threatened with exclusion from school
Mr Mathews	Dom's teacher
Sue	Dom's mother, in her mid-30s. She suffers from multiple sclerosis (MS)*
Chloe	Dom's school friend

The play is set in the present day, at Dom's school and at the house he shares with his mother.

SCENE 1

Dom *is in a school office with* **Mr Mathews**.

Mathews You don't know? [*Pause*] You must have had some reason.

Dom I didn't.

Mathews I wasn't born yesterday.

Dom Could've fooled me.

Mathews I thought we were getting somewhere with you, Dom. You're attendance was back on track, you've been doing wonders with the football team, so Mr Greenwood tells me. Even your behaviour has improved immeasurably. What's happened?

Dom Dunno.

Mathews 'Dunno'. Is that all you have to say?

Dom Dunno.

Mathews *picks up a pile of pink and blue cards.*

* Multiple sclerosis is a progressive disease of the nervous system, which can have many different symptoms. Some people with MS need carers to help them in day-to-day life.

123

DELINQUENT

Mathews   Do you recognize these? They're assault slips, Dominic; pink for verbal, blue for physical. [*Reading from the slips*] We're talking swearing, threatening, fighting, damaging school property. What exactly did you say to Mrs Hibbert?

Dom   Can't remember.

Mathews   Home economics isn't for everyone, Dominic, I appreciate that, but it is simply not acceptable. [*Sharply*] You can wipe that smirk off your face. No one else thinks it's funny. What else do we have? You physically assaulted Aidan Laynes, Andrew Griffiths, Jeremy Spencer and Mr Fish, the school-crossing patrolman.

Dom   They asked for it.

Mathews   They all approached you, did they? 'Hello, Dominic, will you physically assault us, please?' You scratched one of the new bins in the quadrangle, wrote an obscenity in permanent marker on a whiteboard, sent a ball through the biggest window in the science block. What do you think you were playing at?

Dom   Football, sir.

Mathews   Your parents aren't going to be very pleased when we ask them to pay for all the damage. Perhaps I should ring your father right now?

Dom   You'll have to find him first.

           Pause.

Mathews   Do you actually *want* to be excluded? You're certainly going the right way about it. What am I supposed to do? Tell me.

           Dom *stares at the ceiling.*

           There must be some reason you've decided to start wreaking havoc again? Mr Greenwood tells me you're one of the best players he had. Why leave, why now?

Dom   Dunno.

Mathews   Are you being bullied, Dominic? Is it someone on the team?

           Dom *stares at the floor.*

DELINQUENT

You are playing a very serious game here. I can't do anything unless you tell me.

No reply.

It's nothing to be ashamed of.

Dom   It's fine. Everything's fine.

Mathews   If that were true, you wouldn't be standing here now. Mr Hunt wants to know where all of his photo-quality printing paper has disappeared to. You've been using the IT suite most lunchtimes.

Dom   It was for a project.

Mathews   I want to see an improvement. If one more of these slips arrives on my desk, you will be banned from using the IT suite altogether, is that understood?

No reply.

I asked you a question.

Dom   What happens when I've got an IT lesson?

Mathews   You won't have any lessons if you carry on like this. I don't want to see you leave.

Dom   Yes, you do.

Mathews   I'm an inclusion officer. It's part of my job to try and see that you stay here. I've no idea what's behind all this but I'm going to find out. Your behaviour is going to improve and that's all there is to it. You will be sorry if you don't cooperate.

Dom   What are you going to do? Throw one of your slips at me?

Mathews   I'd close my mouth if I were you.

> **Dom** *grabs the slips and tears them all up.* **Mathews** *reaches for a blank slip and starts to fill it in.*

Mathews   [*Writing a slip*] Damaging school property.

Dom   Writing more of them isn't going to stop me. You can stick it where the sun doesn't shine as far as I care.

125

DELINQUENT

Mathews [*Reaching for another slip*] Verbal abuse.

Dom I haven't even started yet. You're an idiot, I've a good mind to give you a kicking. You bloody deserve it.

Mathews Threatening behaviour. Carry on, Dominic.

Dom *grabs hold of him by his jacket lapels.*

I strongly advise you to let go of me.

Dom *tightens his grip.*

Physical assault.

Dom *lets go of him.*

Dom [*Calmly*] I've been doing illegal downloads. I stole a box of CDs from the IT suite as well and you'd better check the lads' toilets in the sports block. There's some really bad stuff written on the wall. You can blame me for that, as well, if you like.

Dom *swaggers out.* **Mathews** *sits in angry silence, shaking his head.*

SCENE 2

Dom *and* **Sue**'s *house.* **Sue** *is sitting at a table, gluing pictures into a huge scrapbook. There is a window behind her. She is crying.* **Dom** *enters.* **Sue** *quickly wipes away her tears.*

Dom Bath's running.

Sue Did you see your girlfriend today?

Dom She's not my girlfriend – how many times!

Sue What's her name, again?

Dom Chloe. She tried to come during break but I made a run for it.

Sue You should ask her round.

Dom Nah, you're alright. [*Pause*] Smells like Mrs Green's been baking again. I might see if she's in, later – what do you reckon?

Sue How do you know it wasn't me?

126

DELINQUENT

| Dom | Very funny. How's it coming on, anyway? |
| Sue | I've just started the nineties. |

Dom *takes a folder from his school bag.*

All the stuff you think you've forgotten. They say you never really forget anything. Everything that ever happens to you is all up there, [*Tapping her head*] you know. It's just a matter of getting to it. Those holiday ones you did came out well. Can you remember that holiday? You must have been, what? Five?

Dom	Eight. It was the first time I'd been on a plane.
Sue	[*Seeing the folder*] Did you manage to get the others done?
Dom	Some.

Dom *hands her the folder.* **Sue** *takes out a collection of photos and some sheets of glossy, thin card with photos printed on them.*

They're fantastic. They look better than the originals.

Dom	I fixed 'em up a bit on the computer.
Sue	Thanks, love. It'd be a shame to stick the actual ones in, they might get damaged. Is it your birthday?
Dom	No, Mum.
Sue	Tomorrow, then?
Dom	No. You've been asking me that all week. Is that why you've been crying – you think it's my birthday?
Sue	It's looking at all of these again. You're growing up so fast. You'll be leaving school soon.
Dom	[*Under his breath*] Sooner than you think.
Sue	So she didn't talk to you?
Dom	Leave it out, Mum.
Sue	You should go out a bit more, you know. Make a few friends. What happened to the lad from football?

127

DELINQUENT

Dom   I got thrown off the team. Coach said I wasn't good enough. I hated it, anyway.

Sue   How was school?

Dom   Fine. You might as well tell me, Mum.

Sue   There's nothing to tell.

Dom   Did the doctor come to see you?

Sue   Yes.

Dom   And?

Sue   It's too early to tell. Shouldn't you be checking that bath?

Dom   Is it stage two? What did he say, Mum? Can you remember?

Sue   It's likely. I'll need to see the specialist before they can be sure.

Dom   I'll give 'em a call tomorrow.

Sue   I'm not totally useless. I can still pick up a phone, love. He said we can get help.

Dom   We don't need it.

Sue   They can send people round.

Dom   What did you tell him?

Sue   Nothing. He wants me to start thinking about the future. You can't stay with me forever.

Dom   We'll be fine.

           Pause. **Sue** *is upset.*

           You're not going in a home. I won't have it.

Sue   That wouldn't be for years.

Dom   As long as they think Nan's still around, we'll be fine. We're doing okay, aren't we?

Sue   What did I do to deserve you, eh?

DELINQUENT

Dom   I did you a CD as well.

            Dom *takes a CD from his school bag and hands it to her.*

            Eighties crap – all the stuff you like.

Sue   When did you do this?

Dom   Today, while I was scanning your photos.

Sue   [*Looking at the hand-written CD cover*] Adam Ant. I used to love him. You've found the Kate Bush one! Where did you get all these?

Dom   Internet.

Sue   I used to love dancing to this. They played it all the time at junior Tiffany's. I must have been about your age.

            Sue *flicks back through the pages of her scrapbook.*

            There we are, look. That's me with Jane Bryan. She'd promised to meet three different lads that night. She was a bit of a goer was Jane, even then.

Dom   [*Embarrassed*] Mum.

Sue   It was huge inside. It's where the bingo place is now on Donny Road. She managed to make all three of those lads believe she was on a date with just them. I kept having to pretend to drag her onto the dance floor so she could nip over and see the next one. It was always mainly girls on the dance floor. The lads never wanted to dance. Do you like dancing?

Dom   No.

Sue   Just like your dad. You're getting more like him everyday.

Dom   I hope not.

Sue   Only in looks. You're worth ten of him, a hundred.

Dom   I can't believe you've remembered all that.

Sue   [*Indicating the photos*] It's these.

Dom   I'll go and check your bath.

            Dom *exits.* **Sue** *stands up – it's a struggle for her. She steadies herself and walks across the room*

129

DELINQUENT

towards the CD player. She moves slowly, almost as though she's forgotten how to walk. **Dom** reappears behind her. He watches as she puts the CD in the machine.

[Softly] You okay?

Sue   Fine.

Dom   Do you want me to help?

Sue   I can manage.

Sue can't get the CD door open. Her movements are slow and deliberate. She tries to press the button several times. **Dom** approaches her. He takes her hand and helps her to press it.

I was pressing the wrong one.

Dom   Which track do you want?

Sue   Number seven, please.

Dom takes her hand and guides her finger to the appropriate button. Music: 'They Don't Know' by Kirsty MacColl. **Sue** tries to dance but is very unstable. **Dom** takes her hands and steadies her while she dances.

Come on, you miserable article, don't just stand there.

Dom starts to dance with his mum. **Sue** loses herself and sings along. **Dom** hides his embarrassment by performing deliberately bad moves.

Sue   You're a crap dancer.

Dom   You're a crap singer.

Sue accidentally stamps on his foot. He lets go of her for a second while he hops around.

Sue   [Still dancing] Sorry!

Dom   Don't mention it.

Sue almost falls over but **Dom** catches her in time. They dance together. **Sue** is laughing but exhausted.

Dom   Come on. I'll dance you to the bathroom.

Dom supports **Sue** as she half dances and half stumbles to the bathroom. The music continues as lights fade.

130

SCENE 3

*It is the next day and **Sue** is lying motionless on the floor. The music from the previous scene fades out slowly.* **Sue** *looks around the room. From where she is, she can see under the table.*

Sue   I'll kill that little sod. How long has that been there?

Sue tries to slide herself closer to the table but can only manage a few inches. There is a knock at the door.

Dom?

More knocking.

You'll have to use your key.

*Chloe's face appears at the window. She is 15, and dressed in a school uniform. She has a brightly coloured envelope in her hand. She peers into the room, and sees **Sue** on the floor. **Chloe** taps on the window.*

Chloe   Hello. Can you hear me?

Sue   Who's that?

Chloe   I'm a friend of Dominic's. Have I got the right house?

Sue   He's not in at the minute.

Chloe   Is the back door open?

Sue   No, love. Try the kitchen window.

Chloe leaves the window. Her voice appears from another direction.

Chloe   [Off] Is it okay if I stand on the draining board?

Sue   Go for it.

The sound of a plate smashing comes from the kitchen.

Chloe   [Off] Sorry.

*Chloe enters the room. She goes straight over to **Sue**.*

What happened?

DELINQUENT

Sue	I fell over, that's all.
	Chloe helps Sue up onto her chair.
Chloe	How long have you been like this?
Sue	Not long. He should be home soon, love. Are you Chloe?
Chloe	How did you know that?
Sue	A wild guess.
Chloe	How are you feeling? Palpitations? Short of breath? Have you got any pains in your chest, at all?
Sue	I'm fine.
	Chloe takes out her mobile and dials.
Chloe	Just try to breathe normally. I'm ringing for an ambulance.
Sue	There's no need.
Chloe	Best get you checked out.
Sue	Don't call an ambulance, please. I know what caused it. It's part of my condition. Please.
	Chloe aborts the call.
	Thank you.
Chloe	Dominic didn't say anything about a condition. You're not having a baby, are you?
Sue	No, love. I can safely say that I'm not having a baby.
Chloe	Dom never said anything about you being poorly.
Sue	It's only now and then.
Chloe	What is it? Do you mind me asking?
Sue	It's called MS.
Chloe	I've heard of it. Muscular sclerosis.

132

DELINQUENT

Sue   Multiple. Not far off, though.

Chloe   Sorry. I don't know much about that one. I'm going to be a nurse.

Sue   Good choice.

Chloe   I used to spend loads of time up at the hospital. One of my mates wants to be a nurse as well. We used to take sandwiches over to A&E and try and guess what everyone had wrong with them. We'd tell each other how we were going to treat them, like it was a medical. She was always better than me – her dad's a doctor. Would you like a drink of water?

Sue   That would be nice.

            Chloe exits in the direction of the kitchen.

Chloe   [Off] I can do a cup of tea if you like?

Sue   Water's fine, thanks. Is Dom expecting you, then?

Chloe   [Off] No. I came to drop his card round.

            Chloe comes back in with a glass of water.

Sue   Thank you. Do me a favour, love. He'll be home soon; don't tell him you found me on the floor, he'll only get upset. Some days are worse than others; this is just a bad one.

Chloe   Are you in remission?

Sue   Remission is when the symptoms go away. What's the card for?

Chloe   It's for Dom. I only found out yesterday. It was his birthday yesterday, wasn't it?

Sue   Yes. [*Short pause*] Sorry, I was miles away.

Chloe   You don't mind me waiting, do you?

Sue   Not at all. It's nice to have another woman around the place.

Chloe   No one's called me a woman before. Are you doing a scrapbook?

Sue   It was Dom's idea. Some people with MS have trouble remembering things, you see. It's just a precaution, really, just in case. He thought it might be a

133

good idea for me to write things next to the photos, while I still know all the people and places. [*Sighing deeply*] I knew it was his birthday.

Chloe   You wouldn't forget a thing like that. [*Looking in the scrapbook*] Is that Dom there?

Sue   Yes.

Chloe   He was a cute baby.

Sue   He was a big baby. Eight and a half pounds.

Chloe   Wow, they're normally between six and seven, aren't they? I was six and a half, my mum said. I suppose girls are smaller than lads. I hope I have girls.

Sue   There's no hurry.

Chloe   Have you had to take time off work, then?

Sue   I haven't worked for a while.

Chloe   Which school was it?

Sue   Sorry?

Chloe   Dom said you were a teacher?

Sue   I worked in a leisure centre.

Chloe   Were you a swimming teacher?

Sue   No, I worked in the café.

Chloe   What are lads like? They'll say anything to try and impress you. [*Pause*] Is he in detention again?

Sue suddenly tenses, controlling her alarm.

Sue   Again?

Chloe   He's always being told off for something. Mr Mathews has been threatening to have him excluded.

Sue   He hasn't said anything.

Chloe   He wouldn't, would he? It's only what I've heard. I think Dom's alright, really. He's nowhere near as tough as he makes out.

DELINQUENT

Sue	You're right there.
Chloe	Does he talk about me much?
Sue	He likes you. He'll be glad you came to see him.
Chloe	That's a relief. You don't mind, then?
Sue	Why should I mind?

The sound of the front door opening.

Dom [Off] I'm back. Sorry it took so long. It was packed, then I had to wait nearly half an hour for a bus.

Dom *enters with several supermarket shopping bags. He sees* **Chloe**.

What are you doing here?

Sue	Mind your manners. Chloe came to see you.
Dom	How did you know where I lived?
Chloe	Trina Banks followed you home yesterday.
Sue	She's got you a birthday card, Dom.
Dom	Why? It's not even my birthday.
Chloe	I know. It was yesterday, I checked. Here you go, it's not a cheap one.

Chloe *hands* **Dom** *his card.*

Sue	I asked you if it was your birthday.
Dom	Don't start.
Sue	You've come home in a great mood. I suppose you're going to tell me you've been excluded now.
Dom	It's the first I've heard of it.
Chloe	It probably isn't even true.
Dom	It's not.

135

DELINQUENT

Chloe	I think it's great the way you look after your mum, like this. I don't know any other lads that'd do all the shopping. I can't believe you haven't told anyone. [*To Sue*] You must be really proud of him.
Sue	I am. Most of the time.
Dom	It was just today. My gran normally does everything. I hardly have to do anything. It's just while she's away.
Chloe	Where is she?
Sue	Australia. She lives there.
Dom	Mum!
Sue	Are you going to open your card?
Dom	No.
Chloe	I think I'd better go.
Dom	Yeah. I think you had.
Sue	Don't be so nasty, Dom. [*To **Chloe***] You can stay as long as you like.
Dom	I know what you're trying to do and it won't work.
Sue	What?
Dom	[*To **Sue***] What have you said?
Sue	Nothing.
Chloe	We were just talking about women's things.
Sue	She'd only been here a few minutes, Dom.
Dom	Who the hell is Trina Banks, anyway? You followed me home, didn't you?
Chloe	Forget it.
	Chloe heads for the door.
Dom	Don't tell anyone.
Chloe	Tell anyone what? Where you live? That you've been to the flipping supermarket?

Dom	Anything.
Chloe	No one's interested, anyway. You're not that important.
Sue	I'm sorry, love.
Chloe	What is it with you?
Dom	I thought you were leaving.
Sue	No wonder no one ever comes to see you, if this is how you treat people.
Chloe	It's nothing to be embarrassed about, looking after your mum now and then.
Dom	What would you know?
Chloe	I'm gonna be a nurse when I leave school.
Dom	So?
Chloe	You want to be excluded, don't you? It's not because you hate school, either.
Sue	Have you been trying to get excluded, Dom?
Chloe	It's because you want to be home all the time, isn't it?
Dom	She doesn't know what she's talking about.
Chloe	Your mum thought you'd be pleased to see me. You always talk to me at school.
Dom	You don't give me any choice.
Chloe	What's so bad about people knowing, anyway? I don't understand it.
Dom	There's nothing to understand.
Chloe	I think there is.
Dom	I don't care what you think. I don't care about anything, okay?
Chloe	What are you so scared of? You can't pretend nothing's happening; you'll have to tell someone sooner or later. The thing your mum's got gets worse, doesn't it? She was on the floor when I got here. She couldn't move. She asked me not to say anything because she didn't want you to worry about her, and she told me about your scrapbook idea. That sounds like someone who does care

to me. Someone who cares a lot, and what's so wrong about that? I knew there was more to you that you were letting on. That's why I wanted to come round.

Dom How long were you on the floor?

Sue Only a few minutes.

Chloe I shouldn't have said anything. Your mum asked me not to mention it.

Dom This is gonna be all round school now.

Chloe No, it won't. You wouldn't believe the stick I got for wanting to come and see you. People think you're weird, did you know that? It was me that followed you home yesterday, but I was too scared to knock. I wish I hadn't bothered. That's called being honest, by the way. You should try it sometime.

Chloe turns to go.

Dom It was my birthday.

Chloe stops and turns to face **Dom**.

Sue Dom.

Dom You'd only get upset again. You haven't been able to go out and get me anything. You wouldn't have known, anyway, if it wasn't for her.

Sue But I did know – I remembered. I asked you if it was.

Dom I'm sorry, alright!

Chloe [Softly] You ignored your birthday so your mum wouldn't have to get you anything?

Dom Don't make a big thing out of it.

Chloe That's so nice.

Sue He is, he's a lovely lad, really. He'd do anything for anyone.

Dom squirms.

Chloe You should ask for help, you know. I'm sure you'd be able to get it.

Dom We're okay as we are. I want everything to stay as it is. We're fine.

Sue	[*To* **Chloe**] Do me a favour, love.

Sue *beckons* **Chloe** *over and whispers in her ear.* **Dom** *stares out of the window.* **Chloe** *exits in the direction of the kitchen.*

She's a nice girl. Are you okay?

Dom	If people find out, Mum, we might have to live in different places.
Sue	Put some music on.
Dom	I'm just thinking about us.
Sue	Listen to your mother. Do as you're told. Something you like, this time.

Dom *looks through their collection of CDs.*

Things might have to change, son. We'll be okay. We've managed so far. We'll talk about it some other time, we've got some celebrating to do. One other thing, you stick chewing gum under that kitchen table again and I'll clout you one.

Dom	Sorry. What are we celebrating?
Sue	You'll see. It wasn't Mrs Green, by the way. She just got me the ingredients. Come on, where's the tunes?

Dom's *music starts playing.* **Chloe** *enters carrying a tray. On the tray is a homemade birthday cake with 15 candles.*

Happy birthday, son.

The music gets louder as **Dom** *blows out the candles and* **Chloe** *cuts the cake.* **Dom** *hugs his mum. Fade to blackout as the party starts.*

DELINQUENT

Class discussion

As a class, discuss what a 'normal' family is. It may be hard to come up with a definition on which you all agree.

In the play, the role of parent and child has, in some ways, been reversed. Dom has a number of responsibilities as his mother's carer. Dealing with these responsibilities brings Dom into conflict with other people in his life.

Draw an outline of a person on a flipchart to represent Dom. On one side of the figure, list some of the things Dom might have to do to look after his mother. On the other side, list some things Dom has to do to look after himself. Do you think that a young person of 15 would be able to cope with these pressures?

Inside the outline, list the things you think Dom is most frightened of.

Group activities

1. Choose someone from the group to play the role of Mr Matthews. The rest of the group are senior teachers in the school who are reviewing Dom's behaviour. Place a chair in the middle of the circle, and 'hot-seat' Mr Matthews about the incident in his office. Try to find out what Mr Mathews thinks might be causing Dom's misbehaviour, and what he thinks the school should do about it.

2. Choose a section from Scene 1 that shows Dom's unruly behaviour. Re-stage the scene introducing improvised lines of dialogue and movement from characters mentioned in the scene, such as Mr Fish or Mrs Hibbert. You might choose to freeze the action and have each actor step into the scene, saying a few lines from the incident directly to the audience. Or you might use a split stage, with Dom stepping out into short exchanges with each of the characters he mentions.

3. Dom's home life is far from ideal. In your group, devise a scene that shows what Dom's home life might be like in an ideal world. Make your drama stylised by adopting exaggerated, cartoon-like characters. Now contrast these images of a 'perfect' family by cross-cutting to sections of the original text.

4. Chloe says that people at school think Dom is weird. In pairs, create an improvisation that shows Chloe and her best friend discussing Dom. Chloe is telling her friend she is going to call round at Dom's house. What does her friend say to her, and what reasons does Chloe give for wanting to go round?

DELINQUENT

5. Dom is helping his mother prepare a photograph album of family snapshots. Why do you think he is doing this? In your group discuss what might be in the pictures? Develop an improvisation that shows Sue sitting alone looking at the photographs. As she turns each page, create a still image that shows a different family memory. Develop the exercise into a short performance, in one of the following ways:
    *   devise a short monologue for Sue to perform as a narration for a series of still images; or
    *   have Sue step out of her chair and take her place in each image, which then becomes animated into a scene lasting a few seconds.

Performing the play

1. In small groups, read Scene 1, the confrontation between Dom and Mr Matthews. Who has the highest status at the opening of the scene? Take turns to act out the opening, with the rest of the group observing as a critical audience. Focus on making the status of the characters very apparent: think about levels, voice, tone, body language, silence and stillness. Does the status of the characters change towards the end of the scene? Identify a point where the status changes. How might you show this?

2. When Dom is at home with his mother we see a very different side to his character. Identify some moments from Scene 2 that show the caring and thoughtful side of Dom's character. Take turns to act out these moments in your group. Do you think Dom feels comfortable in his role as carer, or does he sometimes feel awkward – dancing with his mother, for instance? How might you show this?

Writing

Delinquent touches on a number of themes, including: parent and child roles; school exclusion; children as carers; anger management; actions and consequences; fear of change; living with illness; life choices; memories.

Using the Internet, try to find out what support networks and services are available for people who find themselves in Dom's and in Sue's position. Write a guide for young carers, describing the kinds of responsibilities some young people are faced with, offering advice, and listing and describing the organisations they may find useful. Use headings to divide the guide into topics, and write in short, clear sentences.

141

Boy band

Characters

Andy	A singer in a boy band. Aged 16
Jay	A singer in a boy band. Aged 16
Terri	A girl friend of the two boys. Aged 16

The play is set on the stage of a band competition, a hotel bedroom, Terri's bedroom, and in the lobby of the hotel.

SCENE 1

The finals of a band competition. **Andy** and **Jay** are performing a love song, boy-band style. **Jay** is blonde and cute-looking, **Andy** is dark and muscular. They go into a dance routine.

SCENE 2

The boys move to separate spaces on the stage, and address the audience directly.

Jay   It was the most nervous I'd ever been. It was a live show. The final. We were waiting behind the set while they rolled a compilation of all our best bits. It was down to three acts.

Andy   Me and Jay, a trio of fantastic black girls, and a bunch of guys from the Northern College of Music.

Jay   They did bubblegum covers and made it sound like opera. Yeachh! Nice blokes, though.

Andy   Just for a second the fear left us. We were both standing there in silence but our heads were full of stuff. It's all about luck. That's what I was thinking. It's all about luck.

Jay   Then we were running on. You couldn't hear yourself think for the screaming. The track kicked in and we went for it. Everything came together. The moves, the harmonies. We looked at the right cameras at the right time, we worked the crowd, we were flying.

Andy	It was full on, exhilarating. Like the first time you ever kiss someone, a cross between blind terror and seventh heaven. Is it going to work? Am I doing it right? We obviously were. It rocked.
Jay	We rocked. It was bang-on perfect and everyone could feel it. Before we knew it, there was a whole studio on its feet. We'd done it.
Andy	This was the stuff that only happened to other people. It was happening to us. We were important. People wanted to know everything about us. What we were wearing, who we were seeing. We were told all that. You didn't have to think, yourself. Good job – there wasn't time to think.
Jay	We were told what to sing, what to say, what to wear, likes, dislikes, just about everything.
Andy	It was good, in a way. The lies created space. They stopped people from getting too close. A lot of them think they know everything about you. Most of the time, they don't know anything.
	Their winning song fades back in, to the sound of hysterical applause. **Andy** *and* **Jay** *melt back into the performance, flashing blinding smiles to their audience.*

SCENE 3

Terri is in her bedroom, jumping up and down, clapping and cheering. She catches herself and acts cool.

Terri	[*To audience*] I know them, yeah. We went to school together. I'm cool about it all now. No I'm not. [*Short pause*] I'm so nervous. I've got a 'thing' tonight.

She writes 'DATE' on a piece of paper, then holds it up to the audience.

I don't use the actual word – makes me feel sick. I'm an agony aunt. I started on our school magazine. I work on a website now. I dish out advice on relationships. The really hilarious thing is, I haven't even got one. Bitter, me? I have had a boyfriend – Gary McLoud. He came round last year clutching a bunch of geraniums, 'I've just chucked Kim so you an' me can gerriton. What d'yer fink?' He was seventeen, he had a Fiesta, I thought it was fantastic. We lasted three days. In that time I'd lost my virginity, had my first taste of Woodpecker and seen a real tattoo. 'Kim forever'. I know. This is going to sound so lame but I thought he loved me. I even thought I loved him. I should've saved myself but I didn't, what are you gonna do? You can say 'if only' a thousand times but it never changes anything. The only thing that would sort out the mess that is now my life would be a big, shiny time machine. Wouldn't that be great? I could zap myself back to the moment just before it started.

Terri *points to things in the room as she takes us back.*

...And here we are, in the conservatory. I'm over there, trying to look alluring, Gary's here [*pointing*] ... geraniums, cider. He speaks. 'I love you Terri, you're dead mature, you look like you're twenty or something...', blah blah blah. I wonder how long I could bear it for. Having to stand here and watch me desperately trying to impress. I even took up swearing at this point, in some stupid attempt to appear experienced. Gary speaks again, 'Kim was right stuck up', he shuffles from one enormous foot to another, 'I have to beg before she'll even kiss me.' I just made a stupid snorting noise, so attractive. I speak now, 'She must be frigid.' Yes, I actually said that. He's taking a mouthful of cider, putting the bottle down, lumbering towards me. I'm trying not to look nervous, which is making me more nervous which I'm fully aware of, so I'm doing it all even more and feeling totally stupid. It's unbearable. He's leaning over me. The wicker's creaking under the strain. 'Don't do it!' I'm carrying on. We both are. Clumsy and fumbling. It's truly vile, hideous beyond belief. Oh, please don't say I did that. I can't have thought that was attractive. Too gross. Too gross!

Terri *jumps forward, playing a 'superhero'.*

'Danger, Terri Donahue. Resist! Resist! Gary McLoud is a stupid pig and he's using you for sex.'

Imagine the look on my face, and his. [*As superhero*] 'Put him down, Terri, or shame and humiliation will be yours forever!' You'd scream the place down, wouldn't you? Or you'd just sit there and quietly freak out. 'Oh look, there's me telling me off. I look just like my mother.'

Terri *comes back into the present.*

I didn't enjoy it, any of it. I hated it, in fact, and he chucked me the next morning. He went back to Kim. I know. My mum and dad would have me locked up if they found out. I was fifteen, they'd be disgusted. It's disgusting

BOY BAND

to me. Fifteen means different things to different people. For a lot of them, it's still the age of innocence. We're obedient, well mannered. Clean living, full of potential. When you actually are fifteen, the reality is a lot different. We're afraid and confused and frustrated and guilty and angry and nervous, so very nervous. I shouldn't speak for everyone. Sixteen isn't so different, either. What time is it? Three hours and counting. I don't even know what I'm wearing yet. Every time I open the wardrobe door, the word 'tart' comes screaming out. Maybe I should turn up with a sack over my head. Maybe I shouldn't turn up at all. Maybe I should stop jabbering. There. Stopped.

SCENE 4

Jay is in a hotel bedroom.

Jay   [*To audience*] We've just done a radio interview. We were in another TV studio yesterday. It still feels like someone else's life. We answered questions and had buckets of gunge thrown over us, the usual Saturday morning stuff. One of the viewers was supposed to have written in and asked if I had a girlfriend and 'where was the last place you snogged her?' Judy Crowston from Humberside, aged eight. Eight! I was really embarrassed. I just said that I'd never kissed anyone. The presenter kicked in, 'maybe you can be the first, eh, Judy?' I was obsessed with my Power Rangers when I was eight. The thought of anyone kissing made me want to spit. I got it in the neck for that one. You're supposed to stick to the script. Hardly anything you hear us say in interview actually comes from us. They tell you what to say. They write the questions and give you the answers. And if you get asked something different we have to stop the interview and start it all again. I was supposed to start talking about my girlfriend yesterday morning. I've just started seeing a girl from another band. None of it's true so I'm not even gonna tell you who she is. We've got the same manager, he figured pairing us off would be good for sales. I've never even met her. He's just sorted a magazine interview for next week. The two of us are doing a photo shoot. All this just for saying I've never kissed anyone. [*Short pause*] I hate being a fake. I hate telling lies to everyone, it's wrong. The only way to enjoy any of this is to pretend you're someone else. 'Just go with it', Andy says. He's loved it from the second we won the competition. I have to keep the real me hidden away. He's still in here, somewhere... screaming to get out.

145

BOY BAND

SCENE 5

Andy enters the hotel room but Jay doesn't see him, as if they are not in the same scene. Jay lies on the bed, picks up a magazine and leafs through it without interest. He continues to read the magazine throughout the scene.

Andy   [*To audience*] Jay has always been different. He's dead brainy for a start. He can memorize stuff just by looking at it, and he never swears, it's weird. He uses baby words for body parts, if you know what I'm saying. They've had stylists and life coaches onto him, trying to toughen him up a bit, but it hasn't worked. They gave up after a couple of months and decided he'd just have to be 'the cute one'. I'm supposed to be hard. That's why they have me doing that stupid rap stuff in the middle of the new single. Jay thinks it's hilarious. After the video shoot he came up to me, all serious and said, 'I hope you're going to wash your hands now.' I just looked at him, 'Why?' 'They've been stuck in your armpits for the past five hours, either that or wrapped around your doo dahs.' I was trying to be 'street'.

He performs a couple of the moves, finding them ridiculous.

He had a point, though, it does look a bit on the pathetic side. Wait till you see the video. I got my own back. I held him in an armlock till he came up with something better than 'doo dahs'. I took a copy of the video to my mate Darren in hospital. I thought it would cheer him up a bit. Darren's my other mate. He took a leathering from some fellas outside a club a while back. All the nurses can't believe he'd been getting cards and stuff from a pop star. They went stupid when I first went to see him. 'Andy! Andy!' That's my name, nurses, don't wear it out. It's great. It's like everyone's your mate. The fame thing can be seriously weird, though. People the same age as your mum try it on and stuff. One of the nurses handed me a phone number on the way out. I thought it was so I could call to see how Darren was getting on. Wrong. I've got to tell you something, here. Get ready. The nurse was a bloke. That's not as weird as you'd think. Darren was beaten up because he was gay. The nurse knew all this, Darren loves him, he thinks he's great. I reckon Darren was a bit jealous. He was one of the toughest lads in school, he doesn't look hard or anything, he can't sound hard to save his life, but he's got more guts than any of the idiots that attacked him. He doesn't care who knows. He's never tried to hide it, not even at school. Being gay at school is like having a disease or something. The worst kind. I asked him if he was sure, if he really knew.

146

He said he's always known. It's sort of obvious with Darren. You can tell, if you know what I'm saying. I'm lucky in a sense. I don't look gay, I don't sound gay. There's only three people that know I am.

SCENE 6

Terri's bedroom. She is still getting ready for her date.

Terri Andy looks a bit like Gary. Pop star Andy, my mate? But Andy's got a brain and he's not a pig either. I've fancied Andy since year seven. We were in 'Charlie and The Chocolate Factory' together. All three of us. Jay was Charlie – he always got the lead parts cos he's got an amazing memory. I was Veruca, Andy was Mike TV. He was brilliant. They both were. The three of us have been really close ever since we did the play. I thought my luck was in, not so long back. He came round to see me, this was just as they were getting famous. I couldn't believe it.

Andy appears by her side.

My heart was thumping that hard, I could swear you could see it through my T shirt.

Andy I wanted to ask you something.

Terri [To **Andy**] Great. Go ahead. I am an agony aunt, remember? Virtually unshockable. [To audience] This was it, he was about to beg me to go out with him, and the poor lad couldn't get a word in edgeways. Stop talking now. Stop with the mouth! [To **Andy**] What is it?

Andy Do you think Jay's gay?

Terri Gay? Jay? I don't know. There'd be a lot of disappointed girlies out there if he was. Every girl in the country fancies Jay. Not every girl. I don't. [To audience] Put a sock in it. [To **Andy**] What makes you think he is, anyway?

Andy He has girls throwing themselves at him all the time but he never does anything about it.

Terri He might not be ready. He is only sixteen, Andy. [To audience] Hypocrite, or what? [To **Andy**] I suppose he could be. What if he fancies you? He might. Loads of people do.

147

BOY BAND

Andy	I'd have picked up on it. *[Pause]* There is someone he keeps going on about. A girl.
Terri	There's your answer.
Andy	He won't do anything about it. He's made me promise not to tell her.
Terri	Maybe he's just shy.
Andy	He's definitely shy alright. Hey, you're pretty good at this. *[Pause]* Are you seeing anyone?
Terri	No. Single. Little miss available. Open to offers. *[To audience]* He'd have picked up on it? How far did I have to go?
	Andy becomes apprehensive.
Andy	I shouldn't really be doing this. The last thing I want is for it to spoil our friendship.
Terri	What's the matter?
Andy	I think you should know. I can't say it. Someone close to you, a lad, who... who...
Terri	Fancies me?
	Andy looks very awkward.
Terri	It's OK Andy. You don't have to say any more. *[To audience]* Here it comes, he's being cryptic. Lads always do this. *[To Andy]* Is he from our school perhaps?
Andy	Warm.
Terri	Does he like singing?
Andy	Warmer.
Terri	Was he in 'Charlie and the Chocolate Factory'?
Andy	Boiling.
Terri	Okay. Let's be grown up here, Andy... *[To audience]* Welcome to the second most humiliating moment of my life. He couldn't get a word in. I went on

BOY BAND

and on. How we mustn't take it too fast, how we'd have to be careful of the media. Another time machine moment.

Andy *exits.*

He had no intention of asking me out. You know that, right? I accept you have to get your heart broken a few times, that's just part of the relationship thing. But why does it have to be so humiliating?

Terri *finds the 'DATE' piece of paper. She screws it up, then, after some thought, flattens it out again.*

Nothing is ever what you expect.

SCENE 7

The hotel bedroom.

Jay   When this all started happening, Andy and I promised to keep an eye on each other. If either of us started showing any signs of turning into an idiot, we had to give the other one a hard slap and tell 'em to get a grip. It's easy to forget who you are. It's not that either of us think we're anything special, it's just that loads of other people do. And there's the money. I earn more than my dad. I'm not showing off, by the way, it's just so weird. We play stadiums sometimes. Supporting much bigger acts, obviously. You'd never think it, but it is possible to feel totally on your own, even when you're standing in front of thousands of people. It's because they don't know who I am. More because I think too much, probably. It's hard enough to meet people anyway, never mind with all this celebrity girlfriend rubbish. We can't stand each other, by the way. We're supposed to have been together for three months now. I've just bought her a car and a watch worth three thousand quid. First I knew of it was this morning when I read it in the paper. I'll start believing it all myself soon. I did meet one girl. She was a fan, but different to the others. I used to ring her up all the time. She was dead shy at first, then I told her my girlfriend was all made up and she relaxed after that. She came to a gig. I got her tickets and everything. It was great. For the first time in months I didn't feel lonely. She was out there watching me, this beautiful girl. She came back once when we'd finished the set. We just stood there looking at each other. It felt like an hour before either of us said anything. I went to give her a kiss on the cheek but she really went for it. I mean, really went for it. She thought

149

she had to. She thought that's why I'd paid for everything. Nothing happened. She ran out of my dressing room in tears. She was embarrassed, I suppose. She wasn't the only one. I'm supposed to be a sex symbol, ironic or what? I've never even kissed anyone. Not properly, not someone that I wanted to kiss. I want to love someone. I want my first time to be nice, with someone I really care about. Some sex symbol. That's what you get for pretending to be someone else all the time. You can't get close to anyone. 'Hi, I'm Jay. I'm a liar and a virgin, can I get you a drink?' Not the best chat-up line, is it?

Andy comes in.

Andy   You all set, then?

Jay   Just about. [*To audience*] He's just been to see his mate in hospital. We're flying out to Japan tonight, in the early hours. We've been trying to see as many people as we can. [*To **Andy***] How is he?

Andy   Okay. They say he'll be out in a couple of weeks.

Jay   I thought he already was.

Andy   Very funny. Are you gonna tell me who it is, then, or do I have to beat it out of you?

Andy play-fights with Jay.

Jay   [*To audience*] I've got a date. A real one.

Andy   You haven't got long, you know. The car's coming at eleven.

Jay   Let me go, then.

Andy lets go of Jay. He fixes himself up and makes to leave.

Andy   Good luck, mate. Don't do anything I would.

Jay   No fear of that.

Jay exits. Andy speaks to the audience.

Andy   You can get over fancying someone but you can't stop loving them. My mum told me that. That's what it's all about, really. It's about loving someone. Boyfriend, girlfriend, mate, whatever, and it's not that easy to find. Jay thought me and Darren were seeing each other. We're not, by the way. I told Jay I always thought that he was, or might be. He took it well. He knows who he is, he doesn't need to prove anything. He just needs a girlfriend. A real one. I never had to tell Jay, he just worked it out. He said that if he was a girl and I was straight, or if I was a girl or he was actually gay – that I'd be perfect for him. That takes some bottle for a straight guy. I reckon I know who he's gone to see. We both went to school with her. I hope I'm right. She's fantastic.

Andy picks up a guitar and starts to play. The music continues under the following scene.

SCENE 8

The lobby of the hotel. Terri is waiting for someone.

Terri Don't fidget. Don't pick your nose, play with you hair, laugh like a pig, and above all, don't jabber.

Jay enters.

[*To audience*] He asked me. He's dead good-looking, isn't he? I'd never really noticed before. Too busy chasing after his best mate. And yes, he does know I used to fancy Andy. He's probably all experienced by now, being a superstar and all. He'll probably be after one thing, you know what lads are like.

Jay Hi. I'm really glad you turned up. I'm terrified.

Terri I don't bite. Not on a first date, anyway. I don't do anything on a first date.

Jay Me neither.

Terri Or the second.

Jay I haven't got a girlfriend, by the way.

Terri Good start.

Jay I had to kick off a bit. She's going to finish with me tomorrow. My manager's putting a press release together.

Terri It won't do your popularity any harm. I always preferred my pop stars single. It made you think you were in with a chance. Not that I ever have.

Jay Neither have I.

151

BOY BAND

Terri	You must get offers all the time.
Jay	None that I've taken. I want to tell you something. It's a bit awkward. Do you mind if I tell you a secret?
Terri	[*To audience*] He's bi-, or into something really weird. It's all those groupies. He was lovely and quiet when we were at school.
Jay	I've never had a girlfriend.
Terri	[*To audience*] What did I tell you? Bi-! Remember what Andy said that time?
Jay	Do you mind?
Terri	[*To Jay*] It is a bit strange.
Jay	I was hoping we could just get to know each other, take it slow. I really like you, Terri. I always have.
Terri	Lets be straight with each other. Are you bisexual, Jay?
Jay	Where did that come from? No. Just because I've never slept with a girl, doesn't mean I'm into men all of a sudden.
Terri	[*To audience*] I'm wrong. You can convince yourself of anything if you worry enough, can't you. Did he admit to being a virgin just then?
Jay	Yes.
Terri	Did I say that out loud?
Jay	Yes.
Terri	Sorry. There's nothing wrong with that. It's nice. Not what I was expecting, but that's love for you.
Jay	Love?
Terri	Relationships. They're never what you expect.
Jay	Have you had loads of boyfriends?
Terri	[*To audience*] Here we go. Good bye, future happiness. [*To Jay*] Just the one. It didn't last long. Do you know Gary McLoud?
Jay	No, who is he?

152

Terri	Oh, just some useless, no good, pathetic, pig. I'm over it now.
Jay	So you don't mind then, me being, you know…?
Terri	Not if you don't mind me not being.
Jay	I'm sure I'll get over it.
Terri	[*To audience*] I wish I could.
Jay	Do you mind if we go somewhere else? There's loads of people looking.
Terri	Fine by me.

Terri *beams to her audience then signals to them to clear off.*

Blackout.

BOY BAND

Group activities

1. In your groups, discuss what it might be like to be a famous celebrity or pop star. What pressures are faced by those people lucky – or unlucky – enough to be forever in the public eye? Divide a piece of paper into two columns. Make a list of the pros and cons of stardom.

    Using stylised drama, create a short 'job advert' for members for an all-girl or all-boy band. Think about how some boy bands seem to follow a tried and tested formula in the number of singers and the 'look' of the individuals in the band, the type of songs released and the dance routines. Return to your list of pros and cons and highlight five points from each column. Using these points as headings, create a series of ten-second movement and language sequences that represent each one. You can use the headings as narration. Experiment with different ways of contrasting the negative and positive sides to make a satirical point.

2. Look for evidence in the play that shows the control the band's management has over the band, and over Andy and Jay's lives. Why do their managers want to have so much influence?

    Imagine that it is early in the band's career. They have a successful single in the charts and are regularly appearing on television. In small groups, create an improvisation showing the record label executives sitting down and discussing the band's future. Are they concerned with the artistic and musical element of the band, or more interested in money? Are they concerned with who Andy and Jay really are? In the improvisation, discuss a rumour reported in the press that Andy is gay and that Jay has never had a girlfriend.

3. Secrets are an important theme in the play. In your group, discuss the type of things that young people might keep secret. The characters in Boy band seem to feel guilty about their secrets, as if they think they are 'fakes'. Are they being unfair on themselves? Andy's friend Darren may have ended up in hospital as a result of being open about his sexuality. Why do you think some people react so negatively towards people of different sexual orientation to their own?

    Imagine it is some months later, after the end of the story in the play. Create three short monologues in the style of Scenes 2 and 3 of the play. What has happened to the characters? Have Jay and Terri begun a serious relationship? Has Andy become more open about his sexuality, or is he still keeping it private? Who else might he have told?

Performing the play

1.   Read through Scene 2 of the play. Who are the characters talking to as they describe winning the competition? This technique, of stepping out of the action to talk to the audience, is often called direct address. In your group discuss any examples of films, plays or television when a character speaks directly to the audience. What sort of relationship does this set up with the audience? Do you think it is an effective way of telling a story?

        Experiment with different ways of saying Jay and Andy's lines in Scene 2. Try to capture the excitement and tension of the competition by focusing on:
        *   tone of voice
        *   body language
        *   facial expression
        *   changes in pace

2.   All the characters have a secret which they admit during the course of the play. In Scene 6, Terri thinks that Andy is about to ask her out, but he tells her that it is Jay who fancies her. Rehearse and perform the end of this scene focusing on the way that Terri misinterprets Andy's guessing game.

        Now create an improvised scene of the moment when Terri launches into her 'mustn't take it too fast' speech. How does Andy react? What does Terri say when she finds out it is Jay who fancies her? Does Andy tell her that he is gay?

Writing

        Many young people are very conscious of their image, and anxious about how their friends and peers see them. The powerful need to be part of the crowd, and fit in with what is viewed as 'normal', can steer some young people towards making decisions they later regret. In the play, Terri feels that she is a fake because she gives advice on relationships while making mistakes in her own personal life.

        Read Terri's monologue in scene 3. What advice would you give a girl or boy in her situation? Write an article for Terri's 'agony aunt' column, to a young person who has written in describing a similar experience.

Helen's kitchen

Characters

Helen	A girl hosting a party for her 16th birthday
Julie	Helen's school friend, who has also just turned 16
Paul	A party guest, and school friend of Helen
Matt	Paul's best mate
Cash	An older boy with criminal connections. Julie's boyfriend

The play takes place in the kitchen of Helen's parents' house, on the evening of her 16th birthday party.

SCENE 1

Helen and Julie are in Helen's kitchen preparing party food. The room has one door leading onto a garden and another to the rest of the house. Helen is pouring fruit juice into a large punchbowl.

Julie   That needs more than just juice.

Helen   This is for people who don't drink.

Julie   Like you?

Helen hands her an apple.

Helen   Can you cut this up, please? You don't think he's going to dump me, do you?

Julie   On your birthday?

Helen   All I did was ask him to come on holiday.

Julie   And invite yourself to his dad's house.

Julie cuts the apple in half.

What are you wearing tonight?

Helen   This.

Julie   What about when people get here?

Helen	This.
Julie	You could be one of the best-looking girls in our school if you tried a bit. I can help you if you let me.
Helen	Can you cut that a bit smaller, please – it's going in the punch.
Julie	That's why you asked me to share your party, anyway.
Helen	No, it isn't.
Julie	It's cos you want all of my cool mates to come.
Helen	I've got lots of my own mates.
Julie	Not with any style.
Helen	What about Paul?
Julie	He's not a mate – he's your boyfriend.
Helen	Not for long.

Julie cuts the apple into four and dumps the pieces into the punchbowl.

Julie	He's not going to dump you. I'll make sure of it. Those granny fashions are gonna have to go, mind you. Lads like designer stuff.
Helen	This *is* designer. Someone must have designed it.
Julie	A crusty old nun somewhere. That stuff wouldn't look good on a rubbish tip. Relax. By the time I'm done with you, he's gonna be gagging for it!
Helen	Well he won't get it. Have you and Cash…?
Julie	What do you take me for? We've only been together a week. I might tonight, though.
Helen	Julie, you're sixteen. He's four years older than you.
Julie	I'm seventeen, and so are you if he asks.

The doorbell rings.

That's a bit early. It'll be your library mates – I can hear their pigtails flapping in the breeze.

HELEN'S KITCHEN

Helen exits. Julie takes a huge bottle of vodka and starts pouring it into the fruit punch. Helen runs back in. Julie hides the bottle.

Helen   It's Paul – it's Paul. He's here with Matt.

Julie   Don't let them in.

Helen   I've got to.

Julie   Get upstairs – leave this to me. Go.

Helen exits. Julie pours more of the vodka into the punchbowl. Paul and Matt appear at the garden-side door. Paul is well dressed, in street gear. Matt is a little geeky, wearing a baseball cap back to front. He can't take his eyes off Julie. She hides the vodka bottle.

Julie   You're early.

Matt   You look nice, Julie.

Julie   Yeah.

Matt   Is the doorbell broken? We couldn't hear it. I could fix it – I fixed ours at home.

Julie   It's not broken. Nice hoody, Paul.

Paul   Where's Helen?

Julie   Getting ready. [*To Matt*] What are you staring at?

Matt   Nothing.

Julie   Your luck might be in tonight, you know. Loads of Helen's desperate mates are coming.

Paul   He's not interested – are you, mate?

Matt   No. I already know who I want to go out with. [*Trying to play it cool*] So, Julie, I haven't seen you ages. I've been wanting to ask you something.

Julie waits for the question. Paul offers Matt silent encouragement.

        Is there a downstairs toilet?

Julie   I've got to be somewhere. [*To Paul*] Help yourself to juice.

Julie exits.

158

HELEN'S KITCHEN

Matt	I don't even need to go.
Paul	Some chat-up line that was.
Matt	She makes me nervous. Everything went out my head.
Paul	There's still time.

Matt fills a couple of mugs with punch and hands one to **Paul**.

Just keep telling her how great she looks and try to be funny. Don't say stupid things and remember to wipe your hands on the side of your jeans before you touch her. It rubs all the sweat off.

Matt	There's no chance of that. Julie wouldn't let me touch her with a ten-foot clothes pole.
Paul	What did I say about stupid things? I blame your mum. She should never have married a vicar.
Matt	He's a choir master.
Paul	And how is that better? You and Julie are going to end up together tonight even if it kills me.

Paul puts **Matt**'s hat on the right way round.

Show me how you're gonna do it. Come on. Get it right this time.

Matt	You be Julie.
Paul	No chance. Here.

Paul grabs a mop from the corner of the kitchen and holds it upright in front of **Matt**.

Julie. Bring it on. Show her what you're made of.

Matt	Hello again, Julie. Thanks for letting me to come to your party. You look very nice.
Paul	No.
Matt	Really nice.
Paul	No!

159

HELEN'S KITCHEN

Matt	Bitchin'. You look really bitchin'. I like your hair. It's so shiny it almost looks wet, not greasy though.
	Paul grabs the mop back.
Paul	Watch and learn. [*To the mop*] Wow, will you look at that! All them curves and me with no brakes. Is it hot in here or is it just you? See that lad over there, Julie? He wants to know what you think of me.
Matt	[Impersonating **Julie**] Why doesn't he ask me himself?
Paul	What?
Matt	She might say that. What if she does?
Paul	He's too shy to talk gorgeous girls like you.
Matt	Good one.
Paul	Have you got a boyfriend? … No? Just as well – I might have to kill him.
	Matt gives **Paul** the thumbs-up sign.
Matt	What if she says yes?
Paul	Ask her if she wants another one.
Matt	What if she has, though?
Paul	She hasn't. I asked Helen last week. Come on, you try.
	Paul hands the mop back to **Matt**.
Matt	I was just thinking, Julie, what it must feel like to be the tastiest lady at the party?
Paul	Girl, chick.
Matt	Chicky girl.
	Paul shakes his head in exasperation.
	Your dad must be a thief. He must have robbed the stars from out the sky and stuck 'em in your eyes.
Paul	That's more like it. Keep going.

HELEN'S KITCHEN

Matt   This arm's leaving in ten minutes, you'd better be on it. I'm a bit lost, can I have the directions to your bedroom? Julie! Julie!

*Matt hands the mop to **Paul**. **Matt** grabs his throat and falls to the kitchen floor.*

Paul   What's happened?

Julie enters.

Matt   [Rasping] Help! Julie, I think I need mouth-to-mouth.

Julie   You'll be chuffin' lucky.

Matt springs to his feet and tries to act cool.

Paul   He was just…

Julie   Acting like a moron? [Changing the subject] Is anyone here yet?

Paul   No.

*Helen enters. She's wearing a tiny skirt, loads of make-up and has exactly the same hairstyle as **Julie**.*

Helen   Hi.

Paul stands there open-mouthed.

Matt   Wow, Helen. You look like a streetwalker.

Helen runs out again.

…A nice one.

Paul   Helen!

*Paul goes out after **Helen**.*

Julie   Are you thick or something?

Matt wipes his hands on his jeans.

Matt   I like your hair. You look bitchin'.

Julie backs away.

HELEN'S KITCHEN

Your dad must be an alien cos there's nothing like you on earth. Do you like computers? I built my own. I can build you one if you like.

Julie's *starting to get scared.*

Do you want to go out with me?

Julie	No.
Matt	I can write you a song if you like.
Julie	My boyfriend'll be here any minute. He's twenty and he's got a BMW.
Matt	Boyfriend?
Julie	He's in a gang. If he knows you've been chatting me up, he'll kick your head in. He's twenty.
Matt	Nice garden. There's a pond. I love ponds.

Matt exits. *Julie* *picks up the mop and starts to clean the floor, as if in her own kitchen. She turns the mop upside down and play-acts with it.*

Julie	Hiya. You look dead stressed, babe. Your dinner's nearly ready. Meat pie, gravy, no veg, just how you like it. … What are you looking at me like that for? You're sex mad, you! Pack it in! Cash, no! I've just had me nails done, the glue's not dried yet…
Paul	[Off] But you look fantastic.
Helen	[Off] I look like a prostitute.

Julie *hurriedly swings the mop back down and carries on mopping the floor.* **Helen** *and* **Paul** *enter.*

Julie	I'm mopping the floor.
Paul	Right.

Pause. There's an uncomfortable atmosphere between **Helen** *and* **Paul**.

You look amazing. You look like a totally different person.

Helen	Thanks a lot.
Paul	I didn't mean that. You look dead sophisticated.

HELEN'S KITCHEN

Julie	It's 'Ho Chic'.
Helen	I'm *supposed* to look like a prostitute?
Julie	A classy one. Where does this go?
Helen	In the garage.

Julie slips out into the garden.

	Are you going to finish with me?
Paul	No.
Helen	My dad's already bought you a ticket for Florida.
Paul	I said I wasn't going.
Helen	He likes you – and my mum.
Paul	They feel sorry for me.
Helen	Why would they feel sorry for you? I haven't told them anything. They thought it would be good if we could spend some time together. I'd be on my own, otherwise.
Paul	You could take Julie.
Helen	I want to go with you. Why wouldn't you let me into your house?
Paul	It was a mess. Do you want your present?
Helen	I want a hug.

Paul puts his arms around Helen. Matt appears in the doorway from the garden. He coughs loudly. They pull away from each other.

Matt	I'm sorry. You look really nice. You look like a pop star. Nothing like a…
Paul	[Cutting him off] Okay, Matt.
Matt	Julie's going out with a gangster.
Paul	As if.
Helen	He's called Cash. She met him last week. I'm a bit worried to be honest – he doesn't sound very nice.

HELEN'S KITCHEN

Julie enters from the garden.

Julie   You haven't even met him.

Pause. **Matt** *takes a gulp from his mug.*

Paul   What's a twenty-year-old doing with someone like you?

Julie   I'm dead mature, actually. Anyway, we're soulmates. We're into all the same stuff, music, clothes, everything.

Matt   He's into girls' clothes?

Julie   Drink your juice.

Matt   What sort of music is he into?

Julie   Loads.

Paul   Matt's good at music. He writes songs.

Matt   I started a new one today. It's about a lad who fancies this girl but she doesn't want to know, so he goes on a murdering rampage and ends up in prison. 'Twisted Lover'.

Helen   A ballad, then?

Matt   Rock ballad. Have you got a guitar, Helen?

Julie   No!

Paul   [*Simultaneous*] No.

Helen   [*Simultaneous*] Sorry.

An excruciating pause. **Matt** *starts singing 'Happy Birthday'.*

Matt   Maybe later.

Matt *empties his mug and fills it up again.* **Julie** *catches* **Matt** *staring at her.* **Helen** *looks at her watch.*

Helen   Quarter to eight.

A knock at the door breaks the silence. Everyone runs into the hall.

164

HELEN'S KITCHEN

SCENE 2

> *Later that evening. Pop music and other party sounds drift in from other rooms.* **Helen** *and* **Julie** *are in the kitchen.*

Julie   It's hilarious through there. That Matt lad's got a couple of your library mates up dancing with him. If you call it dancing. The one with the pink cardy's doing stupid little bunny hops.

Helen   Leave them alone. They're enjoying themselves.

Julie   I suppose they've got him off my case. He's been creeping me out since he got here. What's Paul doing with a mate like him?

Helen   They've known each other since year seven.

Julie   He hasn't dumped you, then? I told you he wouldn't.

Helen   You haven't said anything about his dad, have you?

Julie   That he beats him up?

Helen   Julie!

Julie   He can't hear. He's through there with the king of the geek people.

Helen   He's embarrassed about it. He thinks it's going to put me off him.

Julie   He probably only told you so you'd feel sorry for him. I don't reckon it's even true.

Helen   He had bruises all over his stomach.

Julie   What were you doing, to see his stomach?

Helen   We were tickling each other.

Julie   Steady on.

Helen   That's why he wouldn't let me in. He doesn't want me to meet his dad.

Julie   He sounds like a pig, anyway. Paul's the hardest lad in our school; he doesn't need you to fight his battles for him. Lads fight. It's what they do. They like it. It's not your problem, Helen. It's our night, tonight. We're not gonna let it be ruined by stupid lads. We're mates, right? And whatever happens, I always put my mates first.

165

HELEN'S KITCHEN

Helen	Happy birthday.
Julie	Happy birthday.

The girls hug. The sound of screeching car tyres is heard over the music. An engine revs and there are blasts from a car horn.

Cash! It's Cash. He's here! My hair. What's it like? What's my hair like?

Helen	Fine.
Julie	Seventeen, remember. We're…
Helen	Seventeen.

Julie is heading for the garden, then she turns back.

Julie	My middle name's Diamond and my brother's got a nightclub.

Julie runs out into the garden. Paul enters.

Paul	What was that?
Helen	It's Julie's boyfriend.
Paul	He actually exists? That's weird.

Paul hands Helen a little box.

Present.

Helen opens the box. She takes out a multi-coloured, jewelled pendant on a heavy silver-plated chain.

Helen	It's lovely.
Paul	Do you like it?
Helen	[Telling a lie] Yeah. It's so heavy.
Paul	Shall I put it on?
Helen	It doesn't really go with this outfit. There are a few too many colours. Julie's got me done up like a set of traffic lights as it is.
Paul	You'd look great in anything.

166

HELEN'S KITCHEN

Helen   Thanks, Paul. It's beautiful. It's really nice. I love it.

Helen kisses Paul. Cash enters from the garden with Julie attached to his arm. Cash is dripping with gold. He slams a couple of large bottles of spirits on the kitchen counter.

Cash   Right, time to get this place jumping. [*To Helen*] You have to be some kind of model?

Helen   I'm Helen.

Cash   The other birthday girl. Sweet. Very sweet. [*To Paul*] Put it there, bro'. I think I've seen you around.

Paul   You might have.

Cash   You look like you can take care of yourself.

Paul   I do okay.

Julie   He's the hardest lad in our school, aren't you, Paul?

Paul   Dunno.

Julie   He is. Everyone's scared of him.

Cash   Du'n't scare me. [*To Julie*] You never told me you had such hot mates.

Julie   I did her up.

Cash   Smoke?

Paul   No, ta.

Cash   Good job.

Cash takes his last cigarette out and hands the crushed packet to Julie.

Helen   I'm sorry. My parents don't allow smoking in the house.

Cash pauses with the cigarette between his lips. He flicks the lighter and holds Helen in his gaze. He lets the flame go out.

You can smoke in the garden.

Cash   Maybe later.

167

HELEN'S KITCHEN

Cash hands the cigarette back to Julie. She un-crumples the packet and puts the cigarette back in.

Cash   Is this your fella, then?

Helen   Six weeks.

Cash   Still, can't be easy with a girl who looks as good as this one. I bet the lads are round you like flies round horse…

Julie   [Cutting him off] Helen's got a horse. She horse-rides in competitions.

Cash   [To Helen] I'd never have put you two together. Like a bit of rough, do you?

Helen   I like Paul.

Cash swings a punch at Paul's stomach. Paul doubles over. He's in agony. Helen rushes over to him but Paul pushes her away.

Paul!

Cash   I thought he was supposed to be hard.

Julie   He is.

Cash   Could've fooled me.

Paul   I wasn't expecting it, that's all.

Cash   What type of wheels are you into?

Paul   [Still breathless] I want a quad… I've heard they're coming out with a road version soon. Wouldn't mind one of them.

Cash   You want to get yourself a BMW, mate.

Julie   You've got a BMW, haven't you, babe.

Paul   What kind?

Cash   M Series. Sport. I'm gonna trade it in soon. I'm after something with a bit more poke.

Julie   Something to outrun a cop car? Cash gets chased by the cops all the time, don't you, babe?

Cash   This music stinks.

168

HELEN'S KITCHEN

Helen	Sorry.
Paul	What are you into?
Cash	Busta, Tu Pak.
Paul	I went to see Fifty Cent.
Cash	Pussycat.
	Matt comes in, looking sweaty and flustered.
Matt	Great party, Helen. It's rocking in there. I've just been dancing with two girls. One either side – well, they moved all over. Here, here, one there, one there. Can I have some more juice, please, Helen?
Helen	Sure.
	Matt saunters over to the punchbowl. He slurps the dregs from his mug, wipes the rim with bottom of his shirt then dunks his mug in. The others watch with strange fascination. He drinks it all down then sucks in a lungful of air.
Matt	That's better. Thirsty or what.
	Matt tries to act cool.
Cash	What has he come as?
Helen	This is Paul's friend, Matt.
Cash	Something tells me you're not into Tu Pac?
Matt	Not really.
Cash	Busta? Nelly? Sean Paul?
Matt	No chance. That stuff's wack, man. It's just made to get money out of stupid white kids.
Cash	Is that right?
Matt	Yeah. I know loads about music.
Helen	Matt writes songs.
Matt	I know loads about hip-hop. I bet I know more than you.

169

HELEN'S KITCHEN

Cash   You're an expert, then?

Matt   Yeah. Ask me anything.

Cash   Why don't your jeans reach all the way down to your trainers?

Julie   Good one, Cash.

Matt grabs a handful of kitchen utensils and hands them out to **Helen**, **Paul**, **Julie** *and* **Cash**, *who look bemused.*

Matt   Take one of these. You don't mind, do you, Helen?

Julie   What are we supposed to do with these?

Matt sets out a rhythm with wooden spoons on a work surface.

Come on. Everyone.

Helen joins in and everyone, except **Cash**, *reluctantly follows.*

Matt   Hip-hop's got a bit of everything. Remember 'Apache' by the Shadows?

He hums a few bars of the tune.

They built loads on that break. Breaks are banging. That's where break dancing came from. Keep it going. Pick up the tempo. M.C. Matt's gonna freestyle the kitchen.

He starts rapping.

It was the stories of injustice. Wrongly accused. Innocent and driven, given all bad news. The bruthas took it over, showin' they was hard. Mashin up the rhythm, livin' in a prison yard. Work it. Work it. Move it up, Move it up.

Helen continues the kitchen rhythm with **Matt**. *Paul is acutely embarrassed.* **Cash** *looks scornful.*

Next a revelation, the massive elevation. Afrika Bambaataa and the Zulu Nation. Biggin' up the people who'd been poppin one another. Givin' up a reason for the pacifist bruther. Positive taggin', an end to boddy baggin'. Juice-in' it down for the sweet sound rappin'. One time. Work it.

Matt drums out a final phrase then stops abruptly. The kitchen has been stunned into silence.

Cash   [To **Matt**] Faggot.

HELEN'S KITCHEN

Matt *places his spoons down, fills up his mug once more then exits into the rest of the house.* **Helen** *follows him.*

Paul There was no need for that.

Cash Too right. That lad's gonna get a kickin' one of these days. What are you hanging out with a fool like that for?

Julie That's what I said.

Paul He's all right.

Cash He's an idiot.

Julie He tried to come on to me before. Can you believe that? I wouldn't be interested in a kid like him, even if I wasn't two years older than him, which I am.

Paul You could do a lot worse.

Julie I've got too much self respect, thanks.

Cash I need fags.

Paul There's a garage at the end of the road.

Julie I'll go.

Cash hands Julie a twenty-pound note.

Cash Get forty.

Julie Don't be talking about me.

Julie kisses Cash on the cheek and exits.

Cash How do you fancy earning some spare cash?

Paul Don't know.

Cash I could use a lad like you. You've heard of the Empire, I take it?

Paul Yeah.

Cash What is it, then?

Paul A cinema.

HELEN'S KITCHEN

Cash	It's the name of my crew. You do know what a crew is?
Paul	A gang.
Cash	Think you're up to it?
Paul	Dunno.
Cash	Don't know much, do you?
Paul	Will I have to take a hammering?
Cash	[Raising his fists] There's more to this game than using these. You need to use this [he taps his head]. I'm going places. Give it a year and I'll be running this town. Have you seen our tag? A beehive with a big 'E' in the middle? There's one on the side of Next at the Oakdale shopping centre. You do know what a tag is?
Paul	Yeah.
Cash	We're gonna be massive. They'll be everywhere soon. Your old man smacks you around, doesn't he?
Paul	Who told you that?
Cash	You want to stand up to him.
Paul	I do. Who told you?
Cash	She's got a big mouth, that bird of yours. My old fella wouldn't dare lay a finger on me. He knows what he'd get. He's a big bastard, an'all. Hard as anything. Not with me, though. Not anymore, mate. Have you ever had a piece in your hand? A real one? You do know what a piece is?
Paul	No. I know what one is. I've never…
Cash	[Cutting him off] Ultimate power, mate. You're the nearest thing to God with a Magnum in your hand, and I aint talkin' ice cream, son.
Paul	You got one?
Cash	Glove box. I don't like leaving it in the motor. You can fetch it for me if you like.

Paul shrugs his shoulders. **Cash** takes his car keys out and holds them up.

172

HELEN'S KITCHEN

Cash	Can you drive?
Paul	I've had a go in my sister's Punto.
	Cash throws Paul the keys.
Cash	Stick with me and you could have one of your own before long.
Paul	Can I drive it?
Cash	You can sit in it. You can touch the steering wheel. If you so much as turn the engine over I'll rip your head off.
	Paul exits.

SCENE 3

The kitchen, later that evening. Cash takes a gift-wrapped box from his jacket. Matt enters, slipping past Cash to get to the punchbowl.

Cash	Tell Helen to come in here a minute.
Matt	Did you used to live over by St Mary's?
Cash	No.
	Cash takes a pen from Matt's shirt pocket. Matt lets it go, but eyeballs him.
Matt	I'm not gay.
	Matt goes back into the party. Cash removes a gift tag from the present and puts it into his pocket. He writes something on the present and throws the pen into the garden. Helen enters.
Helen	Is everything okay?
	Cash smiles. He hands Helen the present.
Cash	Happy birthday.
	Helen opens the present. It's an MP3 player.
Helen	It's fantastic. I don't believe it. What have you got Julie?
Cash	A surprise.
Helen	[Handing it back] I can't.

173

HELEN'S KITCHEN

Cash	I'll be offended.
	Cash *presses the MP3 player back into* **Helen**'s *hand.*
	You know who you remind me of?
Helen	It wouldn't be a librarian, by any chance?
Cash	Charlotte Church. You've got class you have.
Helen	I can't believe you've spent so much.
Cash	Why do you think they call me Cash? You are stunning, do you know that? You look a lot older than seventeen.
Helen	I find that hard to believe.
Cash	I'd love to see you on the back of a horse. All that gorgeous hair flying behind you.
Helen	I tie it under my riding hat. Can I get you a drink?
Cash	No, ta. Does your liver in.
	Paul *enters from the garden.*
Paul	Julie wants you. She's on the bench by the fish pond.
	Cash *takes out his cigarette lighter and heads for the garden,* **Paul** *stops him.*
	I've got your...
Cash	Later.
	Cash *exits into the garden.*
Helen	What was that about?
Paul	Nothing. You two looked cosy.
Helen	He gives me the creeps. Are you jealous?
Paul	Am I supposed to be?
Helen	No.
Paul	I don't trust him. He's bad news.

HELEN'S KITCHEN

Paul spots **Helen***'s new MP3 player.*

Who got you that?

Helen My mum and dad. You seem angry again. What's the matter?

Paul I asked you not to say anything. He knows about my dad. Julie's fella. She told him, which means someone must have told her, and it sure as hell wasn't me.

Helen I was worried. I wanted someone to talk to.

Paul You could've talked to me.

Helen I'm sorry. I'm really sorry.

Paul [*Looking at the MP3 player*] You can get a hundred CDs on one of these.

Helen You can have it if you like.

Paul Are you gonna give my present away, as well? I'm not a charity case, Helen.

Helen I'm sorry. I shouldn't have said anything. Forget it. It was a stupid thing to say. I should've kept my mouth shut.

Paul Yeah. You should.

Paul walks out, leaving **Helen** *alone in the kitchen.*

SCENE 4

Cash *and* **Julie** *are in the kitchen.* **Julie** *is emptying the vodka bottle into the punchbowl.*

Cash Close your eyes.

Cash places **Helen***'s jewellery box into her hand.* **Julie** *opens her eyes and squeals with delight.*

Julie How much was it?

Cash Three hundred quid.

Julie I love it.

Cash helps **Julie** *put the necklace on.*

Cash I've got you something else, as well.

Julie What is it?

175

HELEN'S KITCHEN

Cash	I wanna know what I'm getting first.
Julie	It's not even your birthday.
Cash	Has to be my birthday, does it? Lets go upstairs.
Julie	No. [*Pause*] What else did you get me?

Cash hands *Julie* a little bag of pills.

Cash	Try a couple. They might put you in the mood.
Julie	I'm not doing it tonight.
Cash	Your choice. There's plenty who will.
Julie	Thanks for the present. I don't want to take them, though.

Cash stares hard into *Julie's* eyes. He takes two pills out of the bag.

Cash	You'll be fine. They're herbal.

Cash feeds both of the pills to *Julie*.

Julie	Do you love me, Cash? A bit even?
Cash	Find us a room and I'll come and show you.

Julie kisses *Cash*. He hardly responds. She exits. *Cash* drinks the last of the vodka from *Julie's* bottle. He takes out a cigarette and heads for the garden, running into **Helen** who is coming inside. She is crying.

Cash	Are you okay, babe?
Helen	We had an argument.

Cash gently puts an arm around **Helen**.

Cash	Was it the present?
Helen	It wasn't something I'd have chosen myself, but it was a really nice thought. He thinks I wanted something expensive.
Cash	It was.
Helen	It's a disaster.

HELEN'S KITCHEN

Cash	I'd be pretty choked if some bloke gave my bird a better present than mine. Has he chucked you?
Helen	No. I haven't told him about yours. I bet you think I'm stupid.
Cash	I think you're amazing.
Helen	I look like a streetwalker.
Cash	You look fantastic. He doesn't deserve a nice bird like you.
Helen	I'm not a bird.
Cash	Woman then.
Helen	I'm horrible. I'm a rubbish girlfriend.
Cash	I bet you're not.

Cash takes Helen's face in his hands. He kisses her. She struggles but his grip is too strong. Paul enters.

Helen	What do you think you're doing?!
Cash	Tell me you didn't like it.
Paul	What's going on?
Helen	You're a pig. I hate you.
Paul	I said, what is going on?
Helen	Paul… Nothing.
Cash	She came on to me.
Helen	I didn't. He kissed me. I didn't have anything to do with it.
Cash	[To Helen] Got yourself into a right mess now, haven't you?
Helen	He forced me.
Cash	Come off it.
Helen	He's making it all up. He grabbed me and forced me to kiss him.
Cash	She's a liar.

177

HELEN'S KITCHEN

Paul   It didn't look like nothing to me. Did you kiss him, Helen? [*Angrily*] Did you kiss him?

Cash   She was only trying to say thanks for her present. Did she show you what I got her? Over there, look.

Paul   That was from him?

Cash   Better than a scabby old necklace, eh, babe? Her words not mine. Man, she's a right little goer, this one. No wonder you were so keen to bed her tonight.

Helen   What? Did you say that? Have you been telling…

Paul   [*Cutting her off*] No.

Cash   Who's it gonna be, then? Him or me, or maybe you want the two of us?

Helen   You're disgusting. You're an animal. Why are you doing this?

              Paul *pulls the gun out of his pocket and points it at* **Cash**. **Helen** *is terrified.*

Helen   Paul!

Paul   Get over here. What happened?

Cash   I can't lie to you, mate. She came on to me. Big time. I was standing here and she lunged. There was nothing I could do.

Paul   She's sixteen. So's Julie.

Cash   Babe, how could you lie to me like that? Tell him the truth, please.

Helen   I am telling the truth.

Cash   Are you trying to get me shot, here?

Paul   Did he force you?

Helen   It was a misunderstanding. Put it down, please.

              Julie *enters.*

Julie   All the bedrooms are locked. There's a mattress in the attic.

Paul   What's that around your neck?

Julie   A present.

178

HELEN'S KITCHEN

Paul	You gave it away?
Helen	No.
Julie	Cash got me it.
Paul	I got that for Helen.
Julie	I don't think so. [*Seeing the gun in* **Paul***'s hand*] What are you doing? He's got a gun!
	Julie starts to panic. **Matt** *enters and sees the gun.*
Matt	Where did you get that?
Paul	He had it in his car. It's a Magnum.
Matt	No, it's not.
Helen	Does it matter what type of bloody gun it is? Just put it down!
Cash	She's got a point.
Matt	Pull the trigger.
Julie	No!
Helen	Don't. Paul, don't. Put it down. Please!
	Cash *creeps towards* **Paul***.* **Helen** *and* **Julie** *are trembling with fear.*
Cash	He hasn't got the guts.
Matt	Pull the trigger.
Julie	Shut up, will you! Are you mad or something?
Paul	I can't believe you gave my necklace away.
Julie	It's mine, thank you.
Helen	I didn't give it away.
Paul	Look on the back.
	Julie *can't read the back of the pendant.* **Matt** *steps in.*
Matt	'To Helen love Paul'.

HELEN'S KITCHEN

Helen	You had it engraved.
Julie	Get it off. Get it off me! [*To* **Cash**] I don't believe you.
Cash	What are you talking about? She must have found it lying around somewhere.
Julie	I never. He gave it to me. He said it cost three hundred quid.
Paul	[*To* **Julie**] Did you see what your boyfriend got Helen?
Helen	He gave me an MP3 player, Julie.
Paul	And I just caught them snogging.
Julie	You've been snogging my boyfriend?
Helen	No.
Julie	How long has this been going on? You don't get MP3 players from lads without doing something for them!
Helen	I think it was supposed to be for you.
Julie	What are you trying to say?
Paul	Will the two of you pack it in! Shut up. Shut it! Bloody shut it!
	Pause.
Helen	[*To* **Cash**] You should feel ashamed of yourself. You're sick. You're an idiot.
Julie	Don't be calling my…
Helen	Shut up, Julie. Shut your bloody face. He's not interested in you, he's hardly spoken a word to you all night. He's just playing games.
	Suddenly **Cash** *rushes* **Paul** *and grabs the gun from his hand. He pushes* **Paul** *to the floor.*
Cash	What a bunch of losers. You think you're all so great. So grown up. You're just kids.
Helen	We don't need to point a gun at someone in order to feel big.
Julie	Paul did.
	Cash *points the gun around the room.* **Matt** *picks up a wooden spoon.*

180

Helen	We don't deserve this. What have any of us done to you?
Julie	You're not gonna shoot me, are you, babe?
Matt	He's not gonna shoot anyone.
Cash	Get a load of M.C. Munster over there.
	Matt steps out in front of Cash, putting himself directly in the firing line. He calmly walks right up to Cash. Julie and Helen can't believe their eyes.
	You're even more stupid than you look.
Matt	Twenty, you say? Twenty. Why are you going out with someone's who's sixteen?
Julie	Seventeen.
Matt	She lied.
	Matt deftly bashes the side of Cash's hand with the wooden spoon and takes the gun away from him.
Matt	My dad used one just like this for his drama group. It might have been the same one, actually.
Paul	Your dad's got a gun, what are you on about?
Matt	It's a replica. They were doing 'Blood Brothers'. It's the wrong sort really, it's too modern. His dad knows my dad. He's the vicar at St Mary's. I couldn't work it out at first, he looks so different. He used to come to our house for singing lessons.
Cash	No, I didn't.
Matt	My dad said he was the best treble soloist he'd ever heard.
Helen	He was a choir boy?
Cash	He's lying.
	Matt takes a folded sheet of paper from his pocket and hands it to Julie.
Matt	There's nothing wrong with that. It's from St Mary's parish website. I fixed your printer, by the way.

HELEN'S KITCHEN

Helen   Thanks.

Julie   No way. No way.

Matt   His real name's Nathan. Nathan Slater. That's his mum's car in the drive by the way. She bought a BMW after Nathan's granny passed away and left them a lot of money. My dad played the organ at her funeral.

Julie   He gave me pills.

Helen   He did what?

Julie   And he even tried to get me upstairs. Choir boys don't do that. You're not a choir boy, are you, Cash?

Cash grabs hold of a kitchen knife.

Cash   Give me the picture.

Julie hands the picture over to Cash. He tears it up. Matt eyes the knife warily, but keeps his cool. The others are frozen in fear.

Matt   He didn't stop stopped singing until he was fourteen. That's late. Treble voices usually go well before then. When did yours go, Nathan? Last year, the year before, maybe?

Julie   No way.

Matt   I make that sixteen, at most.

Julie   You lying pig.

Matt   Put the knife down.

Cash   No chance. You've had it. You're dead.

Matt   There are over forty e-mails in Helen's outbox right now. All waiting to be sent. I've forwarded one of those pictures to everyone in her address book. She's very popular. I even did one for the *Evening Telegraph*. All I have to do is press 'send'.

Helen   My computer's in the study, we're in here. I don't think it's going to work, Matt.

Matt takes out a mobile phone and presses keys on the keypad.

182

HELEN'S KITCHEN

Matt   Bluetooth. 'Helen's PC' Connect! Access Mail … Here we are.

Matt's finger hovers over the keypad.

Unless you put the knife down, choir boy, that picture is gonna be all over town in about five seconds flat.

*Pause. **Cash** drops the knife, with a sneer of contempt.*

Cash   You're gonna be sorry, all of you.

Paul   Why? Are you going to sing to us?

Cash   Idiots.

***Cash** exits into the garden.*

Matt   [*To **Julie***] How many tablets did he give you?

Julie   Two.

Matt   I'll take you to the hospital.

***Cash** comes back into the kitchen. **Paul** takes the car keys from his pocket.*

Paul   Looking for these?

***Paul** throws the car keys at **Cash**.*

Helen   You can take this, as well.

***Helen** throws the MP3 player at him. **Cash** exits.*

Helen   I think you should send those e-mails, anyway.

Matt   There aren't any e-mails. Is there any of that juice left, Helen?

***Helen** kisses **Matt**. **Julie** then kisses him.*

Paul   Does this mean we're finished?

Helen   I don't know.

Julie   Maybe I should go to the hospital.

Matt   This arm's leaving in two minutes.

Blackout.

183

HELEN'S KITCHEN

Group activities

1. Read Scene 1 of the play. Draw large outlines of people on four sheets of paper to represent Helen, Julie, Matt and Paul. Inside the outlines write your early impressions of these four characters. Now read the play to the end. What else do we learn about them? Write down the things you have found out on the outside of the outlines.

2. From Scenes 1 and 2 of the play, up to Cash's entrance on page 167, create a sequence of still images that shows the relationship between:
   - Helen and Julie
   - Matt and Paul
   - Matt and Helen
   - Matt and Julie
   - Paul and Helen
   - Paul and Julie.

   By the end of the play, have any of these relationships changed? Alter your still images to show how.

3. Choose extracts from the play where Cash appears most 'cool', and create still images of the key moments. Use lines of dialogue as narration to accompany the images you create. Now devise short scenes which show the contrasting reality of Cash's life, perhaps at home with his parents. Perform each image from the play followed by a contrasting 'reality' moment you have devised.

4. Why does Cash feel the need to pretend to be something that he's not. What pressures are young people under that might cause them to behave as he does? What is he trying to achieve, and where do his ideas come from? Think of some questions that you would like to ask Cash if he were present in the classroom. In your group, elect one person to go into role as Cash. 'Hot-seat' him, using the questions you devised as a starting point.

5. What does each character learn during the course of the play? Devise a short scene which takes place one year later, on the evening of Helen and Julie's 17th birthday. Try to show how the characters have changed. Cash, of course, must attend the party!

6. Devise a mock TV documentary where a group of anthropologists arrive at a teenage party: 'And here we see the curious mating ritual of the young people of this tribe – teenagers as they are known...'

HELEN'S KITCHEN

Performing the play

Stage the exchange between Matt and Paul, from Julie's exit on page 158 to her reappearance on page 161. The scene has comic potential as the two boys rehearse their chat-up routines, in a kind of comic double-act. Think about timing, and experiment with using the mop as a puppet. Where would you say the climax of the scene comes?

Writing

1. Write extracts from the two girls' diaries on the night before the party. What are their hopes, fears and anxieties? How do they differ from each other?

2. Imagine it is the day after the party. Write a letter from either Helen, Julie or Cash to a close friend who could not attend. In the letter, describe what happened at the party and what your character feels about it.

   Now write a letter from one of the other characters to this same friend. Are their versions of the events the same?

Going nowhere

Characters

Meddy	An angry teenage girl
Lisa	A teenage girl from a privileged background
Jed	A teenage boy who believes he has psychic powers
Carl	An American teenager

The play is set on an adventure scheme for troubled teenagers, somewhere in Scotland. The action takes place over one night and early the following morning, in a field and in a ruined barn where the young people take shelter.

SCENE 1

A field, late on a blustery, moonless night. **Carl** *and* **Lisa** *enter left.* **Carl** *is holding a map and compass.* **Lisa** *holds a torch.* **Meddy** *and* **Jed** *follow. They all carry rucksacks.*

Carl   It's got to be over that hill.

Meddy   What hill?

Carl   This way.

Carl leads the way. They all exit right. Blackout.

SCENE 2

Lights come up again. **Carl** *enters left, still holding the map and compass. This time* **Meddy** *is holding the torch.* **Carl** *stops and looks around.*

Lisa   My feet are killing me. I've got blisters on top of blisters.

Carl   We can't be far now.

Jed   You've been saying that for the past four hours.

Carl   I don't see anyone else taking the map.

Meddy snatches the map from Carl.

Meddy   Right. Where are we?

GOING NOWHERE

Jed	If we knew that we wouldn't be lost.
Carl	We should head back to that old barn.
Jed	What's the point? It didn't even have a roof!
Carl	It had walls. It'll offer some protection.
Meddy	You lot can if you like. There's no way I'm staying out here all night. No way on earth. Not a chance.

Blackout.

SCENE 3

The sound of a howling wind. The glow from a small fire reveals the four of them huddling in the ruins of an old barn.

Carl	We've lost the orienteering module.
Lisa	Who cares? This is ridiculous. We should have a leader with us. Anything could happen out here.
Meddy	We might freeze to death, or get eaten alive.
Carl	Sure, I hear they have killer sheep in England.
Jed	We're in Scotland.
Lisa	[*Hugging herself*] We haven't even got our sleeping bags. We've hardly got anything. They'll find our corpses in months to come, expressions of terror frozen on our faces, huddled together in a pathetic attempt to stay warm. 'News just in, four teenage tearaways perish in orienteering disaster'.
Jed	Give it a rest.
Lisa	It's part of the punishment. They probably want us to die.
Carl	I'm here by choice.
Lisa	It's the government. Their new strategy for dealing with youth crime. They pretend to take everyone on a character-building exercise then leave them all to die. I bet no one made it back tonight. They'll have given us fake maps. The police'll probably come round with sniffer dogs in a few days to find our

bodies. Our parents can all have proper funerals, then. They can wear black and pretend to be devastated when, really, this is what they wanted all along.

Jed   Have you finished?

Lisa   We're being culled. The perfect solution to unwanted offspring.

Carl   We can't be that far. All we have to do is sit tight until the morning. There's nothing to worry about, we'll be fine. What food do we have left?

They open up their rucksacks and look through. **Carl** *takes out an apple and a small bottle of water.* **Meddy** *takes out a can of Coke and a small paper bag containing sweets.*

I have these.

Meddy   Is that it? You had a load of chocolate before.

Carl   I shared it out

Lisa   What have you got, Meddy?

Meddy   Can of Coke and a Sherbet Dib Dab.

Carl   What the hell is that?

Meddy   I've got Space Rocks, as well.

Carl   You have drugs?

Meddy   Don't be pathetic.

Lisa   They're sweets, Carl. They explode in your mouth.

Carl   That's going to help.

Meddy   So's an apple and a bottle of water.

Carl   I got us here, didn't I?

Meddy   A million miles from anywhere. You should have given someone else a chance. Typical American.

Carl   Excuse me?

Meddy   Why, what have you done?

Carl   What did you mean by that comment?

GOING NOWHERE

Meddy	You're bossy. You always think you know what's best when you don't. And you start wars.
Carl	So do the British.
Meddy	Not for ages we haven't, and it was only cos Hitler was being horrible to everyone.
Carl	What about the Falklands?
Meddy	Shut up. You don't know what you're talking about.
Carl	I don't know what I'm talking about? Is this girl for real?
Meddy	Iraq!
Carl	That wasn't just the US.
Lisa	You started it.
Carl	I didn't start anything.
Jed	Will you two give it a rest!

*Pause. **Meddy** opens her Sherbet Dib Dab and gets stuck in.*

Lisa	My teeth are chattering.

***Jed** takes a jumper out of his rucksack and puts it round **Lisa**'s shoulders.*

Thanks.

***Meddy** rolls her eyes and tuts.*

Jed	What's the matter now?
Meddy	I don't know why you don't just ask her!
Jed	Ask her what?
Meddy	He fancies you.
Lisa	No, he doesn't.
Meddy	And you fancy him back.
Lisa	I do not. Why do you always have to embarrass people?

GOING NOWHERE

Meddy	It's cos he saved your life doing the rafting thing the day before yesterday.
Carl	He didn't save her life.
Lisa	He did, actually.
Meddy	'Actually'. It's cos he fancies her, 'actually'.
Jed	I don't fancy her, okay?
Meddy	You're like a couple of kids.
	Meddy sucks on her liquorice stick.
Jed	[*To Lisa*] That must have been terrifying, I'm surprised they didn't send you home.
Lisa	They offered. I didn't want to.
Carl	You fell into the lake. What's the big deal? We had life jackets.
Lisa	I was trapped under the raft. I couldn't breathe.
Carl	You weren't paying attention. We could have lost because of you.
Jed	She nearly died!
Meddy	And our team would have won if Jed hadn't jumped off to pull her out from underneath yours. I can't believe you just carried on.
Carl	I didn't realize what was happening.
Jed	You didn't want to lose.
Meddy	He told everyone to carry on rowing, I heard him. 'She's fine,' he said, 'Keep going, we're nearly there.'
Lisa	You carried on? That's so horrible.
Carl	I was appointed the team leader. It was my duty to get our raft to the other side of the lake.
Lisa	Preferably, with everyone still alive. What a week.
Carl	No one said it was gonna be easy.

GOING NOWHERE

Lisa	Most of us didn't have a choice.
Meddy	I bet the others got back hours ago. I hate this. You're not telling me you asked to come here. No one in their right mind would want to do something stupid like this.
Carl	It's a challenge. My parents thought it would be a positive experience.
Meddy	Your mum and dad made you?
Carl	The decision was mine. It's an opportunity to meet other people my age. People from different backgrounds, some perhaps not as fortunate.
Lisa	Are you serious?
Meddy	He's all talk. He's done something, like the rest of us, but he's too stuck up to tell anyone.
Carl	You can believe what you like. Why are you here?
Meddy	I smacked a teacher. He deserved it.
Jed	What did he do?
Meddy	Hid under his desk.
Carl	And you're proud of that?
Meddy	He deserved it.
Carl	There's never an excuse for violence.
Meddy	Shut up.
Jed	I bet you're wishing you'd stayed at home now.
Carl	She's just angry.
Lisa	Maybe she has every reason to be.
Meddy	I can fight my own battles, thank you.
Lisa	My mum and dad forced me on this. My mum works in a law firm…
Meddy	[*Cutting her off*] Is that supposed to impress us?
Lisa	She'd heard about it from a youth offending team.

Jed	What did you do?
Lisa	I had a party.
Meddy	What a rebel.
Lisa	They were away, for about the fourth weekend running. It was my birthday. I wanted to have a few friends over but they wouldn't allow it. They promised to take me to Paris to make up for it, a trip round all of the art galleries.
Meddy	That's abuse, that is.
Lisa	A gang of gatecrashers turned up. They ended up wrecking the place.
Meddy	Serves them right for leaving you on your own.
Lisa	The insurance company are refusing to pay for the damage. My dad's an art collector. We're talking thousands. They're not covered because I let them all in.
Meddy	I'd have told them where to stick it. Even being stuck in Paris would be better than being out here.
Carl	Paris is a beautiful city.
Meddy	We might get murdered out here. Brutally, horribly murdered.
Lisa	Pack it in, Meddy.
Carl	[*To* **Meddy**] You're sick.
Meddy	There's supposed to be a killer on the loose; they were talking about it in the dorm last night. Didn't anyone see the coppers on Wednesday night?
Carl	Someone had probably stolen something. It's that kind of place.
Jed	It was because that Edinburgh lad had gone missing.
Lisa	He went home.
Meddy	No, he went missing. He'd have taken his stuff with him if he'd gone home, and the other Scotch guy had his number and he never turned up at home.
Carl	Scottish.

Meddy	Scotch, Scottish, makes no difference to the murderer. The 'Grangemouth Killer' they call him.
Carl	Grangemoor. It's supposed be the guy that set the place up a few years ago. A kid got killed under suspicious circumstances and the owner escaped out here to avoid prosecution.
Meddy	Yeah, that's what they were saying. He's never been seen since.
Lisa	No one could survive out here all that time. We'll be lucky to make it through the night.
Meddy	You will, especially with a murderer on the loose.
Carl	He was a survival expert.
Jed	Can we talk about something else, please?
Meddy	Aww, he's getting scared.
Jed	There's a bad feeling out here. Something's not right.
Lisa	You don't say.
Jed	I think that lad is still around.
Meddy	Maybe his body was dumped in here somewhere. And the killer's gonna come back for it when he's hungry.
Jed	He's still alive.
Carl	You're really starting to creep me out here.
Lisa	Jed can sense things. He's psychic.
Carl	There's no such thing.
Lisa	So you only believe in things you can see, I suppose?
Carl	I have faith in God. None of us have the power to see beyond His wisdom.
Lisa	'His' wisdom!
Carl	The dark arts are dangerous. You shouldn't meddle with things you don't understand.

Jed	What's to understand? I see things. That's all there is to it.
Carl	I don't buy it.
Jed	You sound like my folks. They're frightened of it as well.
Carl	I am not afraid. I just don't buy it.
Lisa	But you believe in God?
Carl	Don't you?
Jed	I do.

Meddy *lets out a loud and deliberate yawn.*

I don't go to church. My mum and dad go all the time but I believe in more or less the same thing as them, or anyone else for that matter. We're all searching for the same thing. We don't know the truth because we're probably not ready for it.

Lisa	Isn't that what reincarnation's about? You keep coming back until you've learnt everything there is to learn.
Carl	Our preacher doesn't go for that.
Lisa	There are so many different versions. Who's to say which one is right?
Carl	There is only one God.
Jed	I like to think so. We just call Him by different names.
Lisa	Or Her.
Jed	It's the philosophy that's important, not what you choose to call it.

Meddy *opens her packet of Space Rocks and pours the contents into her mouth. Her eyes widen. She opens her mouth, the others look round to see where the popping noise is coming from.* **Meddy** *pours the rest of the packet into her mouth then takes a slurp from her Coke can. Her eyes widen even more. She stands up and squeals.* **Meddy** *spits the contents of her mouth into the fire. It goes out, plunging them into darkness.*

Carl	You idiot!

Carl *exits, unnoticed.* **Meddy** *makes guttural snorting and spitting noises. A torch beam cuts through the darkness and shines on* **Lisa**'s *face.*

GOING NOWHERE

Lisa	That's done it. I'm sure the wind just got louder.
Jed	You'll be fine, don't worry…
	Meddy *snorts again.*
Meddy	…so long as the Grangemoor pig person doesn't get you.
Lisa	Give me some light, Jed. There's another torch in here somewhere.
	Lisa *rummages in her bag.*
Meddy	I hate this. They should never have sent us out without phones. It's stupid. I could've rung my dad and got him to come and find us.
Lisa	And how would he manage that?
	Lisa *shines her torch on* **Meddy**.
Meddy	He can do anything. He's great, my dad. We're, like, best mates. He's got a massive recording studio in Liverpool.
Lisa	I'm from Liverpool.
Jed	You don't sound like it.
Meddy	She's posh, that's why.
Lisa	I'm not posh. How come you've got a southern accent?
Meddy	They split up. I live with my mum in London. I see my dad at weekends. He knows loads of artists. He used to produce for Atomic Kitten and the Sugababes. He's recording a demo for me. He's gonna try and get me a deal.
Lisa	That's fantastic, Meddy. Where's his studio?
Meddy	Strawberry Fields.
Lisa	In Croxteth?
Meddy	Yeah. It's, like, an old church.
Jed	Give us a song, then.
Meddy	It's too cold. I'll damage my voice.
	There's a dragging noise outside the barn.

GOING NOWHERE

Lisa	What's that? Someone's out there.
Jed	Shhh!
Lisa	Where's Carl?
Meddy	He's not here. He's gone. Something's got Carl. Something's grabbed him and dragged him outside. It's the killer.
Lisa	[*Whispering*] Carl! Carl!
Jed	Shush, listen.

The dragging sound gets louder. **Lisa** *and* **Jed** *huddle together.* **Meddy** *joins them.*

Lisa	It's getting closer.

They sit in silence. **Jed**'s *torch picks out a pair of feet, walking into the barn. A pile of wood is dropped on the ground in front of them.* **Meddy**, **Lisa** *and* **Jed** *scream.*

Carl	What's going on?

The torch beams are trained on **Carl**'s *face.*

I went to get some more wood.

SCENE 4

The fire is lit once again, and the four of them are sitting around it.

Meddy	This isn't funny now. I'm bored. I'm hungry. It's freezing.
Lisa	These could be our last few hours on the planet. It is getting colder. Much colder. Our vital organs will start shutting down soon. It'll all be over. Maybe we should go to sleep.
Carl	We have to stay awake.
Lisa	I'd rather go in my sleep.
Carl	You shouldn't talk like that. Life is a gift.
Lisa	Life is sick.
Meddy	[*To* **Jed**] You should have left her under the raft, given us all a break.
Lisa	What time is it?

GOING NOWHERE

Carl   3.40. We need to keep alert. Anyone know any games?

Meddy   Wink murder?

Lisa   Not funny.

Jed   We'd have to let him win, anyway.

Carl   There's nothing wrong with winning.

Jed   There's nothing wrong with losing either, so long as you learn from it.

Carl   I don't lose.

Meddy   See, I was right. Have you never lost at anything?

Carl   Only this.

Meddy   So what's the biggest thing you've won?

Carl   I was the tri-state swimming champion seven years running.

Lisa   That's comforting.

Carl   I thought you'd be okay.

Jed   He doesn't lose.

         Pause.

Meddy   I won a singing competition once.

Jed   Sure.

Meddy   I did, thank you.

Jed   So when's this new album coming out?

Meddy   Do you want a smack?

Carl   Is that your answer to everything?

Meddy   My dad is in the music industry, thank you.

Carl   Is that why you attacked a teacher?

Meddy   No. He was a snob, like you. He thought he knew everything.

GOING NOWHERE

Carl	You've got a lot of growing up to do.
Meddy	You came here to mix with scum, didn't you?
Lisa	You're not scum, Meddy.
Meddy	He thinks I am.
Lisa	Why did you hit him?
Meddy	He kept picking on me. I was after the lead part in a school play. It was a musical that one of the teachers had wrote.
Carl	Written.
Meddy	He gave it to some posh kid from the top stream, only cos she'd been sucking up to him, silly cow. I'm better than she was, loads better. I told him he'd never get away with it, then he went off on one. Calling me all kinds, saying I was a waste of space. Then he called me Meadow in front of the whole class, and they all started laughing at me. I lost it.
Carl	Meadow?
Meddy	No one calls me that.
Carl	You attacked a teacher because he used your real name?
Meddy	My real name is Meddy. I need the toilet.
Lisa	You can't go out there on your own. I'll come with you.
Meddy	Leave me alone.
	Meddy exits.
Jed	I think I'd be angry with a name like that.
Lisa	I think it's nice.
Carl	Do you really think she can sing?
Jed	I doubt it.
Lisa	Strawberry Fields is nowhere near Croxteth.
Carl	You should know whether she's telling the truth or not.

GOING NOWHERE

Jed   She's lying about something.

Carl   [*Sarcastically*] Right.

Jed   What are you so afraid of?

Carl   It's no use, it doesn't work on me. You don't know what people are thinking and you can't predict the future.

Jed   You're going to have a son. In about twenty years, you'll turn your back on him. Like mine are trying to do with me. And you'll regret it for the rest of your life.

Carl   You don't know anything about me.

Jed   I know you're scared of not being good enough.

Carl   I'm not scared of anything.

Lisa   What about ghosts?

Carl   They don't exist.

Jed   Just like my dad. You could be the same person.

Pause. The wind outside the barn grows wilder.

Lisa   My uncle saw a ghost once. He was on his way back to Liverpool along the M62. It was chucking it down, so he picked up this hitchhiker. The lad started talking about all these horrible accidents, and he was pointing out where they'd all happened as they drove past. It was as though he'd actually seen them all, my uncle said. It really freaked him out. The lad pointed to a part of a bridge that had been mended. He described the accident in every last detail. It was a car and a lorry. The driver of the car survived but his mate in the passenger seat wasn't so lucky. His mate had been thrown across him. The lad was staring straight at my uncle as he told him all this. He said the paramedics had had to cut through his mate's body in order to get to him. While it was right on top of him.

Carl   That is gross.

Lisa   That's what my uncle said.

There's a loud bang on the outside of the barn. They all scream.

199

GOING NOWHERE

Carl	What the hell was that?
Jed	I'll go.
	Jed exits.
Carl	Do you think we should go with him?
Lisa	It's probably just the wind. I'll stop now if you're too scared.
Carl	I'm not scared.
Lisa	My uncle stopped his lorry and forced the hitchhiker to get out. What a sicko, right? Anyway, he carries on driving towards Liverpool, trying not to think about cutting up bodies and stuff when he sees another one. There's no way he was going to stop again, not tonight, but as he got nearer he noticed this one was staring straight at him. Then he saw his face. It was the same bloke he'd dropped off a few miles back.
Carl	No way.
	*Jed comes back in. **Carl** jumps.*
Jed	There's nothing out there.
Carl	It was probably Meddy fooling around.
Lisa	What's with your parents, Jed?
Jed	They think I'm a liar. Actually they don't. They know I'm telling the truth, they're just scared. Their priest recommended a psychiatrist; she arranged for me to come on this. The only way out of it would've been for me to start lying. To pretend I've been making it all up. I wouldn't do that.
Lisa	I'd rather be out here than stuck at home with mine. I'm an inconvenience. The biggest mistake they ever made.
Carl	That can't be true. You're a great person. Surely they can see that.
Lisa	They never see anything.
Carl	I'm sorry I didn't stop the raft. It was stupid.
Lisa	I'd taken off my life jacket. I was the one being stupid.

GOING NOWHERE

*A scream tears through the darkness. **Jed**, **Carl** and **Lisa** jump to their feet.*

Jed   What the hell…?

Meddy   [Off, shouting] Help. Help me!

Jed   [To **Lisa**] You'd better stay here.

Lisa   Why?

Jed   It might be dangerous.

Meddy   [Off] Help! Arrrghh!

Lisa   It came from over there somewhere.

               ***Jed** and **Lisa** run out of the barn. **Carl** stays put. The voices of the others are heard from offstage.*

Lisa   Meddy?

Jed   Meddy!

Meddy   Help!

Lisa   Keep shouting, Meddy. We'll follow your voice.

Meddy   Over here. I've fallen down a cliff or something. I'm slipping. There's nothing
               to hold on to. [She screams] Hurry up!

Jed   It's okay, we're coming over.

Lisa   Hold on, Meddy!

Meddy   I can't! I can't!

               ***Meddy** lets out a loud and terrifying scream. The wind continues to howl around the barn. **Carl**
               peers out into the darkness.*

Jed   It's pitch black out here.

Carl   It sounded like it was coming from this direction.

Lisa   Meddy!

Jed   Meddy!

Lisa   Just try to hold on. We're nearly there.

Jed	Can you still hear us? Try to make a noise.
	There is another loud bang, this time inside the barn. **Carl** *spins round. He can just make out a hooded figure in the darkness. The figure has a coat on back to front with the hood up over its face. It slowly moves closer.* **Carl** *is frozen in fear.*
Lisa	[Off] Over here, I think I've found something.
Carl	Who are you? What do you want? I'm not afraid of you!
	Lisa *screams, offstage. The hooded figure approaches* **Carl**, *arms outstretched like a zombie. It gurgles and moans.* **Carl** *screams. He looks around for a means of escape. He jumps over the fire and runs out of the barn and exits. The figure slopes back into the darkness. There's a thud offstage as* **Carl** *runs into* **Lisa** *and* **Jed***. They all cry out.*
Carl	There's a thing in the barn. A thing with no face. We've got to get out of here. Let go of me!
Jed	It's not safe out here, Carl. Meddy's still missing.
Lisa	Ugh! There's a dead sheep.
Carl	Get off me. Let me go!
Lisa	Carl!
	Jed *and* **Lisa** *enter the barn. They look around, shining the torch into the corners.*
Jed	There's no one here.
Lisa	We should go back for Meddy. Whatever killed that sheep might still be out there.
Jed	It could've been dead for ages.
Lisa	You're the one that said there was a bad feeling about the place. We can't just leave her out there. Come on, we've got to find her.
Jed	Are you stupid?
Lisa	There's someone out there.
Jed	You're getting hysterical.
Lisa	[Hysterically] I'm not getting hysterical!

GOING NOWHERE

Meddy runs into the barn, scaring Jed and Lisa out of their wits.

Meddy   I'm sorry, I'm sorry. There wasn't a cliff. I was mucking about. I didn't mean it. I thought it would be a laugh.

Jed   What do you think you were playing at?! We thought you were dead.

Carl, offstage, lets out a scream.

Lisa   Carl!

Carl   [Off] Leave us alone!

Lisa grabs the torch and shines it out into the darkness.

Lisa   Over here, Carl! Head for the light.

Carl   [Off] Get out of there. Run. Run for God's sake!

Meddy   There's something out there.

Lisa   We've got to help Carl.

Meddy   No way. There's no way I'm going out there again. No way on earth. Not a chance.

Jed   You can stay here, then.

Jed links arm with Lisa's and they venture out. Meddy runs after them.

The wind howls. Blackout.

SCENE 5

Jed, Meddy and Lisa are sitting round the fire. Jed is holding Carl's hat and one of his walking boots.

Meddy   I banged on the barn. It was me.

Lisa   What?

Meddy   Then I put my coat on the wrong way round. I only wanted to scare him. He never bothered to come and help me. I thought I'd teach him a lesson.

Lisa   That was such a stupid thing to do, Meddy.

Meddy   I wasn't to know there was a real murderer out there.

203

GOING NOWHERE

Jed	We don't know that.
Meddy	He's dead. He's got to be.
Jed	I don't think he is.
Meddy	He's nowhere to be seen. He can't have got very far with one of his boots missing, not out here. And what about the Scottish guy? We've had it. We're like sitting dogs.
Lisa	Ducks.
Jed	He's okay.
Meddy	You don't know that.
Lisa	Arguing about it isn't gonna do any good.
Jed	A woman went missing from our village a couple of years back. It was on the telly and everything. I knew where she was. I even knew who'd taken her. What he looked like, at any rate. I begged them to let me go to the police. They wouldn't. They refused to believe it, even after they'd found her. Even after everything I told them turned out to be true. Carl's fine.

The wind continues to howl outside the barn. **Meddy** *sings to herself softly. She has a very good voice.*

Lisa	You've got a lovely voice, Meddy.
Meddy	My dad hasn't got a recording studio. [*Short pause*] I don't even know who my dad is.
Lisa	I didn't fall off the raft.
Jed	You mean…?

Lisa *cries.* **Meddy** *hugs her. Blackout.*

SCENE 6

The following morning. The wind has subsided. **Lisa, Jed** *and* **Meddy** *are asleep. There is a figure standing over them.* **Lisa** *stirs in her sleep.* **Meddy** *wakes suddenly, sees the figure and screams. The other two jump to their feet in befuddled panic. It's* **Carl.**

Carl	It's me.

GOING NOWHERE

The others relax.

Jed   Where have you been?

Carl points out of the barn, into the near distance. The others look out.

Lisa   It can't be.

Carl   Less than a kilometre.

Jed   We've been that close all this time.

Meddy   So much for being psychic.

Lisa   We thought you'd been murdered, Carl.

Carl   I ran for a while and there it was. Who'd have thought it, huh? I told you it was round here somewhere.

Jed   I'll get the stuff together.

Meddy   So you were just going to leave us all to die, then?

Carl   You're still here.

Meddy   No thanks to you.

Lisa   We were looking for you for nearly an hour last night, Carl. What was chasing you? You said there was something out here?

Carl   The little guy, the one who came after me in the barn.

Meddy   Did you get a look at him?

Carl   His head was covered.

Lisa   'His'?

Lisa looks to Meddy, who looks shifty.

Meddy   Maybe there wasn't a murderer, after all. I suppose we'll never know.

Lisa   You sounded terrified.

Carl   I wasn't.

Meddy   'Course you was. You ran far enough.

205

Carl That's not far. I'm not afraid of anything. I just figured it was a good time to find a way back.

*Jed comes back from the barn with everyone's stuff. He hands **Carl** his boot. The others take their rucksacks and head in the direction of the camp. **Carl** follows, he's limping.*

Blackout.

Think about the way people see you. What words or phrases would they use to describe your personality? Is this how you see yourself? There are many ways to show the outside world who we are, or how we would like to be seen. The words and phrases we use, our body language and attitude, the clothes we wear, can all offer clues.

Unfamiliar situations make us vulnerable, by revealing our true character rather than the image we try to project in our everyday lives, but they can also help us to learn about ourselves. Outdoor activity courses are often designed to encourage people to explore their inner feelings, develop relationships and learn to rely upon each other.

Group activities

1. Look for clues in the script that refer to why Meddy, Lisa, Carl and Jed are on the adventure scheme. Write down a key quote for each character that sums up their story. Discuss in your group if you think the reasons each character gives is true. Did Carl really volunteer for the course? Was Meddy's attack on the teacher as bad as she describes it? Using the quote as a scene title, create short improvisations that re-enact these events. Make two versions of each scene: first, as the character described it; second, what you think really might have happened.

2. Now you have learnt something about the characters, create a short improvisation that shows the team leaders at the activity centre getting ready for this latest group of troubled teenagers. What are the plans for the week? Which of the characters do they think will pose the most problems? Which of the characters do they think is most vulnerable?

3. In your group ask two people to take on the role of Lisa's parents. Place two chairs in the middle of the circle, and 'hot-seat' Lisa's parents, asking them questions about the party incident. Try to discover why they feel their daughter let them down so badly. Do the parents bear any sort of responsibility for what happened? Pose questions that encourage the parents to account for their own decisions. Would the party have happened if the parents had not left Lisa alone over her birthday? Does this in some way explain Lisa's behaviour?

   During the raft race Lisa took off her life jacket and may have jumped in the water on purpose. Ask Lisa's parents about this. Complete the hot-seat exercise by offering advice to the parents on how they might support and help Lisa resolve her issues.

Performing the play

1.   The play develops dramatic tension in a number of ways, as the night closes in on the lost walkers. What role do the stories about the 'Grangemoor Killer' serve? What about the tale of the hitchhiker? Read the stories in your groups in a variety of ways, to find the most effective way of performing them.

2.   If your performance space allows, explore different ways of using stage lighting to create the effect of a glowing campfire. Beyond this dim circle of light, there is darkness. Experiment with using handheld torches to cut through the darkness. If you cannot achieve a blackout in your space, what different ways can you find of suggesting the darkness beyond the campfire?

3.   Look at the opening scenes in the play. How do the characters relate to each other? How would you show the relationships between the characters through language, movement and their positions on the stage? Who has the highest status during these opening scenes? Does their status change? In your group, choose a section of dramatic action to explore. Focus in detail on making the status and relationships clear to an audience.

When you have rehearsed and performed this section, include some improvised moments where the characters step out of the action and say what they feel about each other.

Writing

At the end of the play all the characters have exposed – whether or not they admit it – a vulnerable side to their characters. Imagine that as part of the concluding day of the adventure course, all the characters have been asked to write a letter to themselves. In it they are to describe what the course has taught them about themselves and the way that other people see them. Write the letter of one of the characters in the play. Will your character admit to having been changed, or will they maintain that their experience has not really affected them? What are their plans for the future, and how will they relate to their families when they return home?